THE RIGHT MOVES

THE RIGHT MOVES

Succeeding in a man's world without a Harvard MBA

CHARLENE MITCHELL

THOMAS BURDICK

Macmillan Publishing Company

New York

Macmillan Publishing Company
866 Third Avenue, New York, N.Y. 10022
Collier Macmillan Canada, Inc.

Library of Congress Cataloging-in-Publication Data

Mitchell, Charlene, 1950–
    The right moves.
    Includes index.
    1. Executive ability.   2. Success in business.
    3. Women executives.   I. Burdick, Thomas, 1950–
    II. Title.
    HD38.2.M57   1985   658.4'09'024042   85-15345
    ISBN 0-02-585410-0

Macmillan books are available at special discounts for bulk purchases
for sales promotions, premiums, fund-raising, or educational use.
For details, contact:

Special Sales Director
Macmillan Publishing Company
866 Third Avenue
New York, N.Y. 10022

10   9   8   7   6   5   4   3   2   1

Designed by Jack Meserole

Printed in the United States of America

CONTENTS

Part Three ADVANCED STRATEGIES: CORPORATE BRINKSMANSHIP

Part One

THE CORPORATE

ENVIRONMENT

1

THE NEW EXECUTIVE WOMAN

The feminine advantage

W HY CAN'T a woman be more like a man?"
When a baffled and desperate Henry Higgins posed this question in *My Fair Lady,* women were quite different from men. A woman's place was in the home; and a man's role was to provide for her. While a woman may have been worldly-wise, she was also wise enough not to let it show. But that was in another century and, in many respects, another world. It is now the end of the twentieth century. For the first time, women are working side by side with men, competing with them for promotions, and casting an eye toward the same top management spots.

We believe that as women's roles in the world have changed, there has also been an inevitable and inexorable movement toward shared values, beliefs, and thoughts on the part of the men and women in business. With the merging of male and female roles, a latter day Henry Higgins would be incorrect to think that today's businesswoman is so very different from her male counterpart.

A recent study has shown that successful women in business are quite similar to successful men. They share many of the same characteristics, and are more alike than they are different. Ellen Fagenson, a researcher at the State University of New York, studied 260 businesswomen from different levels. Her results show that the women who are rising fastest in corporate America simply are not bringing traditional "feminine" traits and values to their positions.

Instead, these successful women (22 percent of them high-level managers, and 35 percent of them middle-level managers) "exhibit attitudes traditionally assigned to men regarding their careers." Even more to the point, women who have remained at lower levels are more "feminine"—more committed to family and home.

THE ULTIMATE CHAUVINIST TAKES A BIG STEP

The number of women entering the ranks of business has grown tremendously in the last decade. Consider that in 1973, women were outnumbered twelve to one in the entering class of the Harvard Business School. At that time, a woman at any level in management was unusual. In 1985, however, 30 percent of the Harvard Business School's entering class were women. Clearly, the business environment is changing, and so is the potential for women in business.

In the past, the founder of a family-owned company would hope for a son to someday assume control of the business. But today, the heir apparent may just as easily be a woman. One of the most famous and surprising examples of this was Hugh Hefner's decision to make his daughter president of the *Playboy* empire. If there was ever a man you would expect to dismiss the idea of a woman running a major corporation, you would think it would be Hefner. And yet, the ultimate chauvinist had no reservations about grooming his daughter to take control of a multi-million-dollar conglomerate.

Politics aside, can anyone conclude that Margaret Thatcher is not every bit as savvy and astute as the men in her government? In fact, she is called the "Iron Lady," a term used as a compliment to her political and intellectual strength. Or consider Thatcher's apparent antithesis, Mary Kay, the frothy founder of the cosmetics company of the same name. She has the strategic insights, toughness, and managerial skills to match any of the top auto executives in Detroit. (Maybe more, considering that her company has never operated in the red.) Look beyond the pink Cadillacs and the diamond tiaras and you find a highly profitable and professional organization with an immediately identifiable culture. Mary Kay understood the value to corporate growth of a strong "corporate culture" years before Peters and Waterman even thought of writing *In Search of Excellence*.

IT'S TIME TO GET DOWN TO BUSINESS

Perhaps one of the most important factors to the success of women in business lies in the understanding that both men and women encounter problems in their careers. In many respects, women face the same work-related problems that men do. Yet, if you peruse many of the magazines and books designed to help women in their careers, you realize as we did that they treat women as if they are completely different from men. Most guides are filled with endless stories of women having difficulty of one type or another in business, but they never make the point that men have many of the same problems. From these readings you receive the erroneous impression that only women are naive, only women make mistakes, and only women are confused by the mechanisms of the business world.

This advice, rather than encourage, often only discourages women. The subtle message is that their male counterparts, unencumbered by their innate inexperience, naiveté, and ignorance, are scrambling easily up the proverbial corporate ladder. While they, burdened by problems, assumptions, and thoughts that are particular only to women, are doomed to failure.

"BIOLOGY IS DESTINY"

The biggest impediment to your career is the belief that you are different from your male colleagues, or that you are somehow disadvantaged. This type of thinking is not only a hindrance, but it is incorrect. Men are just as naive, just as confused, and encounter basically the same problems in business that women do.

We are not saying that there are no barriers to the advancement of women in business. They exist and will continue to for some time. But most of these real impediments are in the upper levels. You should realize that while some of the rules of business may be stacked against you, these obstacles are offset by definite, positive advantages in the corporate "struggle." Women professionals are in great demand in virtually every industry today, and they carry high visibility within their organizations. Consider that women graduates of the Harvard Business School Class of 1984 received an average of five offers in their chosen career area, compared to three for the men. This is just one of many positive effects resulting from changes in societal and governmental attitudes toward women since the 1960s.

There *are* differences between men and women. But a woman's destiny is more the result of environment, upbringing, and education than her "biology." And the hard, competitive business environment is tough on both sexes. You should realize that a supposedly astute businessman can be misunderstood by his boss just as easily as a woman can. Or that his position can be undermined by a personality conflict with his secretary. These are the kinds of psychological shackles that often hold women back, and one of the major purposes of this book is to eliminate them.

For this reason, although *The Right Moves* is designed for women, we use stories involving both men and women in business. And why we interviewed men such as Citibank's Chairman Walter Wriston, David Rockefeller, General Motors president Eliot Estes, among others, to get their views on success.

We have also included stories of well-known people and companies in the book to illustrate certain points. It may be enlightening to know that "Sally Jean" was fired from a "certain unnamed company" because her boss just didn't like her. But in our opinion it is both enlightening and encouraging to know that Lee Iacocca was fired from Ford Motor Co. for the same reason.

THE ROUTE TO THE TOP

There are as many routes to the top as there are people at the top. What works for one person may not work for another. You must find your own path to success. This book is not meant to give you the definitive formula. It doesn't exist. But it is meant to get you to think before you act. To reflect, after you have acted. Being successful is a continuous interactive process in which you are the key participant.

While there are no simplistic paths to the top, we do know that there are some decisions and actions that can enhance your chances of getting there. And the more you know, the better your chances of succeeding. English philosopher Francis Bacon once wrote: "Knowledge itself is power." It is also a prescription for success in any endeavor. To this end, we've culled stories, insights, and examples from people and companies who are successful, as well as those who are not.

A CYNIC'S VIEW

While some may call our insights cynical, we prefer to call them realistic. The business world is a hard place, and its rules for survival and success are demanding. Those who think otherwise should reconsider. But many opportunities exist, and great rewards await you if you master the game.

As a woman in business today, you have a better chance of getting ahead than ever before. Some barriers still exist but they are constantly being eroded. And while most successful women today are at the middle-management level, they are moving upward rapidly. Each woman who secures a higher management position will, to paraphrase Neil Armstrong, have made "one small step for woman, one giant leap for womankind."

2

CORPORATE CULTURES:

A WORLD APART

Of suits & saunas

W<small>HAT BEGAN</small> as the simple acquisition of a small company by a larger one, turned into a headline-grabbing event that had business pundits predicting everything from success to disaster. The attention didn't result from the fact that the large company was IBM, the blue behemoth of the computer world. Or because the small company was Rolm, one of the most successful young companies in Silicon Valley, California. The real question that had captured everyone's interest was, as one observer put it, "Are three-piece suits and saunas compatible?"

CORPORATE MICROCOSMS

The two companies epitomize very specific cultures. And more to the point, the two cultures are the complete antithesis of one another. IBM represents eastern establishment business at its most conservative. Managers invariably wear dark suits, ties, and white shirts. (More trendy executives sometimes show their independence with a blue shirt, now that the once ironclad white shirt rule has been relaxed.) Employees work long hours, breaking briefly for lunch and then return to their desks. Long before Rolm was even an idea, IBM had perfected a form of corporate indoctrination in the spirit, philosophy, and style of being an IBM employee.

Rolm, specializing in telecommunications, is the consummate West Coast high-tech company. It is known throughout the "Valley" as the "Country Club," which in itself is quite a distinction considering the free-spirited atmosphere of Silicon Valley in general. Its facilities include an enormous recreation center complete with two swimming pools, saunas, Jacuzzis, and tennis courts. Company policy provides a three month vacation for every seven years of service. Employees wear jeans and polo shirts to work and many spend their lunch time having a leisurely swim in the company pool, followed by a relaxing dip in the hot tub. They set their own hours and no one keeps an eye on the time clock.

While the jury is still out on the IBM-Rolm marriage, it is this contrasting corporate style, or culture, that created near panic at Rolm when the two merged in late 1984. These young managers were keenly aware of the fact that if Rolm is compelled to emulate the IBM culture, they would be both out of place and miserable. And while it may be difficult to comprehend (who doesn't dream of a company in which you set your own schedule and spend your lunch time luxuriating in a Jacuzzi?), the managers who are happy and successful at IBM would feel just as disconcerted if they are transferred to Rolm. The respective employees have selected a company in which they feel comfortable with the business style, the people, and the accepted routes to success.

If there is any universal secret to success in business, it lies in understanding that every company is a world unto its own. Every organization has its own "culture," with standards, rites, and customs that define both the work and the workers. Understanding your company's culture is fundamental not only to your success there, but also to your career in general.

Too many people see the business world as being comprised of a group of uniform organizations. In this simplistic view, the principles that govern success at one company appear to be essentially the same as those of other companies.

No consideration, therefore, is given to the thought that the principles of success may differ from one consumer products company to another, or for that matter, from one industry to another. The end result of this faulty reasoning is the belief that following one set of rules will promulgate success; or that individuals who are successful at one company will be able to duplicate their success at any other.

Such thinking has been disproved time and again. While the general principles of success may appear similar, in application and practice they vary dramatically. You need only to consider the countless stories of individuals who were "hot" at one company and suddenly seemed to lose their "golden touch" when they moved to another, to suspect that there is more to the story.

LOSING THE GOLDEN TOUCH

John was a production manager at a major manufacturing company for over five years. During that time he advanced so rapidly that he was considered a superstar. He was held in high regard by his superiors, who usually lavished praise on his work. It seemed to many, including John himself, that he could do no wrong—that he had the golden touch.

It was then that an executive recruiter contacted him with an offer from another company. The position provided more status and a significantly higher salary. The offer was so attractive that John couldn't turn it down.

Almost from the beginning, however, things started to go wrong. Seemingly trivial incidents at first, but as time went on John's boss paid less and less attention to his ideas. At meetings, his suggestions were acknowledged perfunctorily and ultimately ignored. And it seemed to John that the harder he worked, the worse things became. After a year, John resigned. With great bitterness, he attributed his problems to a personality conflict with his boss and to "circumstances."

Culture shock

The reason for sudden failure following job change, as typified by John's case, is far less mystical than luck, or a "personality conflict" with a superior. More often than not, people are simply unaware of the fact that the "success principles" operating at the new company are different from the old. Consequently, when an individual follows his or her previously successful style, it doesn't necessarily generate the same results. Look at John's case.

John's first company was an old-line firm with a long history of success in its industry. It competed in a stable market. The managers treated business in a slow and cautious manner. Even minor issues were subjected to exhaustive analysis and attention. Moving up in the company resulted from deliberateness, attention to detail, and deference to the chain of command.

In his new job, John continued to act and perform, both consciously and unconsciously, in the style that had previously brought him success. Unfortunately, John's new company had evolved a culture that was radically different from that of his former company. The new firm was young and competed in a rapidly expanding field. Up-and-coming executives here made fast, often "seat of the pants" decisions. In this atmosphere, John's manner of careful consideration of the issues was seen as indecisive. The more he tried, the more he was perceived as weak and ineffectual. To his new boss, he just didn't have the "right stuff."

Out of "sync"

John didn't fail in his job responsibilities. His downfall was his failure to understand cultural differences. He lost effectiveness when he was so obviously out of "sync" with the company's personality. Such examples of culture shock are common. They can seriously derail, and sometimes even ruin, a career.

One basic principle of success, then, is to fit in with your corporate culture. Some people are fortunate to fit in naturally. Their style and personality are in harmony with the company. For these people, like John at his first company, difficulties arise only if they move to a new culture and fail to adapt. Others, however, who do not naturally fit, must learn to mold themselves into a personality that is reflective of their company. Adaptability, while difficult to learn, is an invaluable aid to success.

Of course, if you don't fit and you don't want to adapt, you can move to another company or industry. But, changing firms is not necessarily the panacea for cultural conflicts. It is the rare individual in management who will not pass through many different divisions or areas of a company on the way to the top. And each division may have its own unique cultural flavor. Inevitably, as you progress through a career, it becomes necessary to learn to adapt.

DECIPHERING THE CODE

Unfortunately, these operating rules are not always readily apparent, and it is this subtlety that presents such a great challenge to those who want to succeed. How do you go about learning these cultural factors and rules if each company is its own microcosm?

Some of the more general operating rules of a company are clearly delineated for all. They may be written in company manuals—for example, policies pertaining to work hours or sick days, or to a broad code of ethics such as those prohibiting stockbrokers from trading with insider information. These rules are made known to each new employee and only the most naive would choose to ignore or openly flout them.

But these written codes reveal little about the inner workings of the company or the intangible operating principles that are essential to career survival. Generally speaking, it is not the written codes that create problems. Rather it is the unwritten rules and customs that can throw a career into a tailspin. And these customs constitute the core of a company's personality. Deciphering the "culture code" is fundamental to success at any company.

The right "fit"

The importance of cracking the culture code lies in the fact that success is simply not the result of merely doing a good job. In the business world, success is a very subjective matter. Management's perception of you is much more important than the actual quality or quantity of your work. How well you mesh with your company's culture will have a greater effect on your image. No matter how good your work may be qualitatively, if you are out of sync, you have little chance of going anywhere in your company.

Take the example of Christine, a Harvard MBA who joined a brand management company that had a dominant "macho" culture. People were aggressive, almost brash, in their approach to work, play, and life in general. Christine worked hard, but she had a much more subtle and refined approach to both her work and her life. She also suffered from what was to be a serious drawback at this company—modesty. Because she didn't "toot her own horn," she found herself overshadowed and outpromoted by her more overtly aggressive peers.

Fortunately, Christine realized that she did not fit in and saw that her career was suffering because of it. She switched to another brand management company whose culture was more attuned to her style, and moved ahead quickly.

Industry differences

Just as there are cultural differences between companies, there are also differences between industries. Behavior, style, and outlook that might propel you to the top in one industry could very well be disastrous in another. Many sales- and marketing-oriented companies encourage aggressive and competitive behavior—in work, in the marketplace, and at after-work company activities. Yet, at many banking institutions, particularly those outside of New York, outward displays of such competitiveness would be unacceptable, even though beneath the surface an equally competitive spirit may exist.

This does not imply that every aspect of a company's culture is unique. Some behavioral factors are universal. But even they are not immediately apparent since they, too, are unwritten. Success ultimately requires you to be in tune with most, if not all, aspects of your company's culture.

Corporate personality

The simplest way to determine your company's culture is through observation. Whether or not you are aware of it, you have been assessing organizational cultures and attempting to mesh with them all of your life. When you entered school, you learned the unwritten rules. You observed how the majority of students acted and you assimilated the predominant behavioral styles. The same process holds true in business.

UNIVERSAL CULTURAL FACTORS

Most companies have two types of cultural factors, those that are virtually universal and those that are particular to the company. Together these factors determine the "personality" of a company.

Let's consider those factors which are so prevalent in American industry that they can be called "universal."

The role of the boss

At the most basic level, companies are organized into "boss-centered" clusters of increasing importance. Each group or cluster is relatively self-contained, with the boss managing the group's activities. Those under the boss are expected to implement and carry out the boss's overall goals. No one is expected to perform projects for another boss without express permission of his or her own boss. Nor is anyone expected to complain to another boss, or go over the boss's head.

While there are variations in this boss-centered cultural factor, it is universal in American business. The concept appears quite simple, but it is often overlooked or underestimated. Many prospective employees have failed to grasp the real significance of this principle before their first day on the job, and as a result, make unfortunate job selections.

Tim was a recent Wharton Business School graduate with two years of experience as a financial analyst. He was contacted by a recruiter who informed him of an opening with a New York firm. After a series of interviews, he was offered a senior analyst position in the firm's Budgets & Analysis group, with a substantial increase in salary.

Tim was very excited about the offer. The company had a strong reputation, and the controller was a dynamic individual with whom Tim had established an immediate rapport during his interview. While he was considerably less impressed by his prospective immediate superior, the department manager, Tim allowed his enthusiasm for the controller and the company to sway his thinking. He accepted the offer.

Within a few months Tim realized that he had a problem. His boss had started his career as an auditor, working his way up without the benefit of an MBA. He resented Tim's Ivy League academic credentials. And much to Tim's dismay, he found he had little contact with the controller, who left the running of the group to the department manager. Tim rarely met with the man who was most responsible for his acceptance of the position.

Understanding the boss-centered concept would have made Tim take a second look at the job offer and realize that it was not as attractive as it seemed. Employees rarely interact with managers above their immediate supervisor. In Tim's case, it was the department manager, not the controller, who would have the greatest impact on his progress at the company. In retrospect Tim acknowledged that had he fully realized this, he would not have accepted the position.

The chain of command

The boss-centered factor is closely related to the "chain of command" cultural factor, and together they help to demystify some of the workings of companies. Chain of command is a military term referring to the fact that power and responsibility are directed up and down, level by level, in an organization. At no time does the line of power or responsibility skip a level, in either direction. Nor does it move laterally.

The use of this term, chain of command, in describing business is quite apt. For while these principles are not formalized as they are in the military, they function in a similar fashion. It is enlightening to view the typical office situation from this military-like perspective.

Often employees fired from white-collar jobs because of problems with their boss wonder why someone above didn't come to their assistance. The chain of command discourages intercession into a manager's prerogatives. Upper-level managers rarely interfere with the managerial prerogatives of their subordinates; even if it means that good people at the lower level are underused or, perhaps, terminated.

BUCKING THE CHAIN OF COMMAND   This also explains why it is difficult to go over the boss's head. For those managers weaned on the chain of command concept, this principle must be preserved. To tamper with it goes against the corporate grain. Just as upper management will not break the chain of command underneath them, it is expected that those in lower management will not break the chain of command above them. Consequently, no matter how justified you think it may be, going over the boss's head is a risky proposition.

This principle shows itself in another way. In the military, the head of a unit usually takes all the credit, and the blame, for the accomplishments and mistakes of his outfit. He expects the loyalty of his subordinates, and in return, he offers them stability in the organization. In business, the boss usually assumes similar prerogatives. To the neophyte it is quite upsetting when the boss takes total credit for a project that was completed successfully with minimum input from the boss. Yet, it is a normal outgrowth of the chain of command principle.

Women are especially susceptible to resentment on this point. When the boss claims credit for their work, they may feel that they are being exploited, and that a strong response is required to "set things straight." While some response is appropriate if this continues or goes beyond certain bounds, most of the time this is merely standard procedure.

Class distinctions

Another universal cultural factor is one of class distinctions. Just as society has different classes, so does the corporation. But instead of the rich, the middle, and the poor classes, the modern corporation consists of the executive/white-collar, the blue-collar, and the clerical classes. And the barriers among them are just as real.

As is true in society as a whole, these business class distinctions serve as a considerable barrier to the specific individuals involved. For example, no matter how competent or experienced a secretary may be, she is virtually stuck in that class, outranked by any member of the white-collar class regardless of how "green" and inexperienced the white collar may be.

One does not have to look far to see the effects of this cultural factor on today's corporation. Each class has its own identity, way of dress, and rights and privileges.

THE BLUE COLLAR CLASS   Blue collars constitute a large block of the work force at many companies, especially those in manufacturing. The blue collars may, or may not, be represented by a union, but their rights are distinct from other classes. They must be treated uniformly, they cannot be expected to work more than the allotted time without additional pay; and they cannot be fired without good, usually legally justifiable reasons.

Compared to the blue collar, those in white-collar jobs have far less security. (Henry Ford II fired a white-collar employee simply because he didn't like the cut of the man's suit.) Managers are not represented by any collective bargaining powers and they can be fired fairly easily. Yet, their upside potential is considerably greater than that of the blue-collar worker. Advancement to upper management brings with it considerable power and prestige that is not available to any other class.

THE 9-TO-5 CLASS   Secretaries and clerical workers form another clearly defined class, also characterized by distinct dress, behavior, and performance criteria. While the secretaries work side by side with white-collar workers, a significant barrier exists between them.

Even if a secretary knows everything that is going on in the department and could probably run it entirely on her own, she must still be subservient to her white-collar superiors. And earn considerably less money for her efforts. The most a woman in this situation can expect is a sop such as an "executive assistant" title. Such are the ramifications of class distinctions.

MAINTAINING CLASS BARRIERS   Loyalty to one's business class is often as strong as loyalty toward the company, and there are many different ways of expressing solidarity. Eating lunch or socializing after work together are some ways. Dress is another.

The white-collar male works in a suit and a tie not because it is particularly practical, but because this serves as the uniform of his class. For many years at IBM the male executive's uniform had to include a white shirt. No other color was acceptable. This policy was instituted not because upper management had an irrational predilection for white shirts, but because the uniform had to be maintained.

It is also easy to understand why the emerging business-woman class, in the middle and late 1970s, latched on to the drab masculine business suit—it was necessary to distinguish themselves from the secretarial class. (Seventh Avenue fashion designers had not yet realized the lucrative potential for professional yet stylish clothing for women.) Prior to that time, the typical place for a woman in business was behind a typewriter.

THE REPAIRMAN WHO WOULD BE KING Dressing against class can create problems. The secretary who dresses too much like a professional woman or the blue-collar worker who wears a tie to work may not be breaking any written rules. But they are risking problems on a much more subtle level, in the form of peer resentment. They are, after all, turning their backs on their class.

Consider the service repairman from Sears who wanted to make a good impression on his superiors. He began to wear a white shirt and a tie to work, atypical dress for those in the service department. At first, his colleagues teased him about his clothes. But he ignored the real intent behind the so-called teasing and continued to wear the symbols of management. He was soon ostracized by the other blue-collar workers.

His tactic also failed with management, who sent word down from Olympus that he should dress like the rest of the repairmen. His strategy lost on both counts. His co-workers were antagonized because he was disassociating himself from them. And the managers were annoyed because he looked like them, but wasn't.

SOCIALIZING OUTSIDE OF ONE'S CLASS Socializing outside of one's class can also cause difficulties. While there would appear to be no particularly valid reason why they shouldn't, it is rare to see classes mix. Secretaries will eat lunch with each other and go to after-work spots together. But, the white-collar worker who joins them on any regular basis is risking his or her credibility and long-term image within the company.

Loyalty

Another universal cultural phenomenon concerns loyalty. When one joins a company, more than just a day's work is required. Superficially at least, one is also expected to pledge allegiance to the company. Naturally, this loyalty includes not passing secrets to the competition, but we are referring to loyalty in spirit as well as substance. This psychological allegiance takes the form of talking about "us" versus "them" when speaking of the competition, and shows itself in other subtle forms of language and deed.

On one level, it seems that most employees are making a fair trade with the company: their labor in exchange for a paycheck. But the company demands and expects more, and this goes to the root of this cultural factor. Being an employee is, in many respects, being part of a tribe. Just as a member of a tribe shares a common bond and owes psychological loyalty to the tribe, so does the employee with his or her company.

This "tribal" loyalty is the reason why many companies will immediately dismiss an employee who is discovered to be looking for another job. It is viewed as a rejection of the tribe. If an individual is seen not to be in the right spirit with the organization, it can stall a career.

Origins of universal cultural factors

No one knows exactly how these universal cultural factors developed. Certainly no one consciously designed and applied them to American business. Some are rooted in human nature. Others have their origins in the early part of this century as American industry grew from small enterprises to large corporations. At that time strong, charismatic, and paternalistic individuals such as Rockefeller, Carnegie, and Sloan headed corporations. Their employees, who were in every other respect adults, were often relegated to child-like roles in these big patriarchies.

But despite their murky beginnings, these cultural factors affect in a powerful way the methods and behavior of business. Just as with the common law of England, where custom eventually became law, the customs and habits in organizations have also been solidified over the years. Understanding them forms the basis for plotting a long-term success strategy in business.

3

GREAT EXPECTATIONS

Career reward factors

WHEN STEVEN JOBS, the co-founder and chairman of Apple Computer first met PepsiCo President John Sculley, he was certain that the executive was right for his company. The only problem was that Sculley was quite satisfied with his position at PepsiCo. Despite several attempts and offers of more money and perks than could be had at PepsiCo, Jobs still couldn't entice the superstar marketer to the No. 2 spot at Apple. But he was determined.

Finally, after some thought, he knew what it would take to get Sculley on board. He made one phone call and gained a new president for his company. When asked how he finally swayed Sculley, he replied, "I just told him that he could continue to sell sugared water to children, or he could change the world a little."

Sculley is a dreamer, in the best sense of the word. And so is Jobs. At 43, John Sculley had an outstanding track record and was firmly entrenched in a strong and powerful position. And he had a handsome salary and perks to accompany it. He simply wasn't looking for just more money or power. Sculley may not even have realized that he wanted more out of his career—until Jobs offered him a dream—to play a role in the computer revolution. And despite all the traditional rewards that could be gotten at PepsiCo, Sculley could never really hope to have any significant impact upon society or the world while there.

WHAT BUSINESS REALLY OFFERS

The perceived potential of a career in business has attracted ever-increasing numbers of people in recent years. Most are attracted by the expectations of rewards such as money, power, and prestige. Yet few people really understand the nature and limitations of these "reward factors." And fewer still are aware that different careers in business offer dramatically different rewards.

In this chapter, we will discuss those reasons above and beyond the most basic purpose of a job—economic survival. In one sense, any other reason for working is a luxury.

In his famous delineation, the psychologist Abraham Maslow asserted that there are five levels of human needs. The most important center on the attainment of such basics as food, shelter, and clothing. Only after a person has satisfied these necessities does he move on to other, less vital, needs. In Maslow's scale, the last and fifth level sought is self-actualization, or simply, achieving the goals one sets for his or her life.

People competing for management positions are going to be motivated by factors other than having enough money to purchase food, shelter, or clothing. With their education, background, and talents, these aspiring managers are seeking goal fulfillment. And they expect their jobs to provide this.

REWARD FACTORS

Since economic survival is not the determining factor in job selection, it is clear that these rewards, or reward factors, feed the ego in one form or another. Each person seeks ego confirmation in a different way. For John Sculley it was the prospect of shaping the future that enticed him to leave

PepsiCo, not money or power. (And given the potential of the microchip revolution, Jobs was not being unrealistic.)

The most popularly perceived reward factors in business fall into the following categories:

Money
Status and prestige
Power and influence
Personal freedom and control of one's destiny

Let's take a critical look at how corporations meet these reward factors.

Money

The most common expectation from a business career is money. More to the point, "big money." In general, people in white-collar positions are upwardly mobile and seek salaries that will enable them to live on an above-average scale. Many people at all levels of business nurture dreams of making it to the "big time," especially those just starting careers.

But not all managerial salaries are equal. Some industries offer more money than others, regardless of the similarity in responsibilities and hours worked. A partner with one of the Big Eight accounting firms has the opportunity to make much more money than a banker with the same number of years experience at one of the large national banks.

The person who wants to be rich should consider carefully the industry in which to compete. The odds are against someone becoming rich by pursuing a career in banking or publishing. With some notable exceptions, these fields will only provide enough money to be comfortable, albeit sometimes quite comfortable.

Other careers such as consulting, investment banking, and securities offer much better chances of attaining impressive salaries. Freshly minted MBAs are being tempted with starting salaries of about $70,000 at consulting firms such as the

Boston Consulting Group and Bain & Company. Some of the larger investment banking houses such as Morgan Stanley and Goldman Sachs are offering starting salaries in the mid-60s. This is only the beginning for those who are successful.

THE TAKE AT THE TOP   This is not to discount the substantial salaries garnered by those who reach the top of any industry. John Gutfreund of Phibro-Salomon (formerly Salomon Brothers) took home $2.5 million for his services. And Roger Smith, the chairman of General Motors, earned $1.5 million in 1983. But it must be remembered that these are the top salaries, and the same companies are nowhere near as generous to those even a few rungs below.

STARTING SALARIES ARE DECEPTIVE   Starting salaries in different industries vary and often have little connection to a field's long-term earning potential. This point is frequently lost on the graduating college or business school student considering job offers. Many make career choices based solely upon starting salary offers, expecting that these salaries are an indication of even more money as one progresses in the field.

It is well known that creative people in advertising agencies often begin with salaries far lower (earning about $15,000–20,000) than those of their college or graduate school peers in other industries. Within a few years, however, and with some winning ads, a "creative" in an agency can command a low six-figure salary. Sales is another position that can be low paying initially, but offers lucrative monetary compensation after a few successful years.

TRADEOFFS   Another consideration in the quest for big money is the tradeoffs with other reward factors. For example, there are industries which consistently pay impressive salaries, such as consulting and investment banking, right from the start with new recruits. But these industries also exact their "pound of flesh" for that salary. Even entry-level consultants, for example, have very little non-working time.

Many find that their weekends are spent on airplanes flying to and from clients. While they are making an excellent salary, they have little time to enjoy it or their personal life.

Stockbrokers can earn six-figure salaries after five to ten years. But, even with these large salaries, they are severely limited in the amount of time they have away from the job. Long lunch hours are infrequent, and many are afraid to take even a two week vacation for fear of losing clients. Thus, as in other careers, there is often a big disparity in reward factors.

In some fields, the initial accumulation of wealth takes place at the expense of status. Some examples of this are in the entrepreneurially oriented endeavors: sales, stock brokerage, and commercial real estate. Quite often at the start of a career in any of these areas, there is little status in comparison with a position at a major corporation. Consider commercial real estate. It can be an especially lucrative career with time, but at the entry level confers little status.

Michael, an ambitious MBA from the Harvard Business School, had to endure the bemused smirks of his "B-school" classmates when he opted for a "declassé" real estate career in New York City. Within five years, Michael's net worth was slightly over a million dollars. His classmates, who had pursued more traditional business school careers, were averaging approximately $70,000 annually. At Harvard's Fifth Year Reunion, Michael noticed that none of them still looked down on his career.

While Michael's initial, and only, goal was to make "big money," he ultimately acquired status by virtue of his wealth. This phenomenon occurs quite often. If a person makes a lot of money, he or she automatically gains status, regardless of the career. Today, money can buy just about anything, including respect.

Nor should it be overlooked that the top two incomes for corporate executives nationwide in 1983 went to entrepreneurs. Frederick Smith, founder of Federal Express, received $51 million, and Charles Lazarus of Toys 'R' Us took home almost $44 million.

This simply emphasizes the importance of looking at any career from a long-term perspective.

SIC TRANSIT GLORA MUNDI   Finally, it must be remembered that those big salaries at the top are precisely that, salaries. When you no longer have the position, either by your choice or the company's, you no longer have the money. While a chief executive officer may live like a truly wealthy man as a result of his salary and perks, he usually will be forced to live much more modestly when he is "dethroned." There are few people in any level of an organization who can live well without a salary for an extended period of time.

The rare exceptions to this are some savvy future-thinking executives who ensure when they are hired that they are given "golden parachutes" in their contracts, designed to provide a tidy fortune should they lose their positions. For example, golden parachutes are frequently used for top executives in preparing for a corporate takeover by a hostile company, in the event they subsequently lose their jobs under the new owners.

William Agee, former CEO of the Bendix Corporation and husband of Mary Cunningham, picked up over $4 million from his parachute after he lost his company in an ill-conceived and poorly executed takeover bid of Martin Marietta in 1982. Other lower-level Bendix employees were not so fortunate in the aftermath of Agee's debacle.

Nor is a successful tenure a requirement for receiving a golden parachute. Charles Knapp, former chairman of Financial Corporation of America, led the company into disastrous financial difficulties with his high-risk growth strategy. But while federal regulators were pumping billions of dollars in loans into the ailing corporation to keep it from bankruptcy, Knapp was comfortably vacationing in Europe on his $2 million parachute.

But parachutes are rare, and usually only very senior executives get them. Most executives, even high-level ones, are directly dependent upon their salaries to maintain themselves and their families in the style to which they have become accustomed. All too often, loss of salary means a dramatic decline in lifestyle.

Status and prestige

Status is another powerful career "carrot." It can be evinced by a job title, a prestigious company name, or an impressive field of business.

When Felix Rohatyn, a partner at Lazard Freres, accepted the chairmanship of the New York Municipal Assistance Corporation in 1975 at a salary of one dollar a year, he was obviously trading salary for status. The new position afforded him fame, glamour, and high-powered visibility that few financiers could ever achieve. He later made the cover of *Newsweek* magazine for his efforts to save New York City from bankruptcy.

Even the geographical location of one's office (New York City, San Francisco) can convey status. Status could be a large desk or an elegantly furnished office. For many, status is its own reward. This is particularly true for those who can only perceive their own glory in the reflection of another's eyes. To them, appearances matter more than reality.

THE TITLE TRAP   One industry which is rather notorious for conferring status without financial backup is the banking field. Banking, more than most other industries, suffers from status oriented "title inflation." There is an old cliché about banks that they would rather give an employee a vice-president title than an increase in salary. Obviously this is an exaggeration, but it is close to the truth in many banks. In banking, as in most corporations, the hierarchical pyramid is very wide at the low and middle levels but narrow at the top, despite the impressiveness of the titles at each level.

In the past, if you were the type who liked to add a title to your name or if you felt a title enhanced your identity, then banking was a good career choice. Much of that still exists in the industry today. After the level of vice-president, however, it is difficult to proceed to the next step—a senior vice-presidency, where the salaries in banking really begin to open up. Regardless of titles, the same career bottlenecks and barriers exist as in other fields.

GLAMOUR INDUSTRIES   Banking is just one of the industries that exemplifies the reward tradeoff of status in lieu of a big salary. In other industries, status may take the form of the nature of the business rather than one's title. Take, for example, the broadcasting and advertising industries, which are considered by many to be glamourous. The salaries in both are lower than for comparable positions in other industries for just this reason.

Since few people are confident enough or strong enough to require only their own respect, they need to have it confirmed by others. Most companies are cognizant of this, and use it to their advantage. Referring back to Maslow's hierarchy, this need for respect can be stronger than the need for other goals, such as money or power. Consequently, many employees will accept status in lieu of a larger salary.

THE "NAME" COMPANY   Another form of status is the "name" company. In this instance, one gains status via the halo effect. The principle of the halo effect maintains that if a company has a reputation for excellence, then any employee of that company must also be impressive. Consequently, a person working for Procter & Gamble will receive the satisfaction of being bestowed with the qualities that make the company great. It also is no coincidence that P&G's starting salary offers to graduating MBAs are less than those of most other companies.

Those who bask in the reflected glory of their company will often turn down positions that offer far more advantages and rewards. Consider IBM. Many employees there are constantly offered substantial salaries by other companies, yet they remain at IBM because they prefer the status and ego gratification of working for "Big Blue."

Power and influence

Some people seek careers that bestow power. In business, power usually takes one of two forms: power over people, or decision-making power. For some, true power exists only to the extent of the importance of decisions that they are allowed to make autonomously. For others, simply being able to tell even one subordinate what to do will feed their need for power sufficiently.

Power is perhaps the most misunderstood of all reward factors. In the corporate hierarchy power is often more illusory than substantive. While many people believe that a real power position in a company is tantamount to that of a seignior, most, if not all, of an executive's decisions are subject to major checks and balances. Even the ultimate power of hiring and firing is tightly regulated. Only a few executives in unusual situations can make a decision or implement an action without regard for the input of others.

THE LIMITS OF POWER   Power over the daily actions of others is limited as well. Managerial positions do afford one the opportunity to exert some control over the actions of others, but for the most part, that control is restricted. A typical middle manager may have thirty or forty people in his department, but he also has three or four lower-level managers who directly supervise those people. And while he can monitor and direct all of his subordinates, the chain of command principle dictates that he must do it through his immediate subordinates. Hence, even this power is diluted by being filtered through others.

Even at the top levels, the concept of power is usually misconstrued. It may appear that the CEO directs the activities of all of the corporation's employees. But in actuality, his power must be directed through a handful of top-level managers or division heads. These people have their own power needs, and jealously guard their prerogatives. As a result, the typical corporation head controls only those managers who report directly to him. And like others in the corporation below him, he will rarely break the chain of command to exercise his power.

"TYRANNICAL" LEADERSHIP   As we mentioned previously, the low-level employee who breaks the chain of command to go above his boss's head is often penalized. It is interesting to note that the manager who breaks the chain of command in an effort to extend his power down into more levels of the organization also generates a negative image. These lapses of company protocol are frequently viewed as "tyrannical" and "dictatorial." Consider the case of J. Peter Grace, 71, the chairman and CEO of W.R. Grace & Company, a six billion dollar chemicals and consumer products conglomerate.

Grace, undoubtedly because he is a direct descendant of the company's founder, became its top executive at an early age. (He has held the top spot for thirty-nine years, a record for the head of an American corporation.) As a result of a very aggressive personality, he exerts more than normal influence at every level of the organization. He is notorious for breaking the chain of command and insinuating himself into the activities of employees at levels far below his own. His excessive authority must be endured because of his entrenched position. Other top-level executives, without such a power base, would encounter much greater resistance and limitations to the use of their power.

Personal freedom and control of one's destiny

It is generally conceded that companies require a degree of uniformity among their employees. This is especially true of companies with very strong, well-defined corporate cultures such as IBM, Morgan Stanley, and Delta Airlines. In fact, it is this conformity that contributes significantly to the efficiency and success of these organizations, but it comes at a price.

Many of us take for granted the freedom that being an American brings and attempt to apply it to the business world. But corporate life does not necessarily adhere to the same philosophies. The decision to pursue a career in business often requires the relinquishing of much freedom. This realization eventually sinks in, usually when one wants to do something and finds that he or she is blocked by the "norms" of behavior in the organization.

Consider, for example, that most professionals spend half of their waking day, five days a week, on the job. If they want to take a day off to relax, they have to ask permission. If they show up late, they must offer a reason. If they decide to leave in the middle of the day, they must clear it with the boss. Freedom, in the sense of control over one's time, is quite restricted in most organizations. In this respect, even the small-time shop owner has far more freedom of action than the $100,000-a-year manager.

Or consider the degree of freedom permitted an employee in how to dress, act, or even where to live. Again, being part of a company requires compliance with the restrictions and expectations of the organization. Of course you can dress as you choose, and live in an unchic part of town, but don't expect to get very far in the company. Freedom of personal expression must also be sacrificed in the climb up the corporate ladder.

Pursuing the point a bit further, consider the concept of freedom of speech within the organization. While you won't be banished to Siberia for saying what you really think, your career could well be put into a deep freeze. Do you really have the freedom to tell your boss that his idea suffers from a profound lack of native intelligence? Or that you find some of the company's most cherished philosophies and policies foolish?

A GILDED CAGE   Amanda, a successful Los Angeles stockbroker, mentioned freedom and money as the main factors in her career choice when we talked with her recently. While she does indeed command an excellent income ($100,000+) from her commissions, and she can conduct her business affairs as she chooses, Amanda's freedom is actually far more limited than she perceives. Despite her love of travel, she is not free to take long vacations. She must always be in contact with her office, and in regular touch with her clients. Only twice in the past ten years has she taken two consecutive weeks' vacation, a schedule hardly conducive to extensive travel.

Amanda is also very limited in choosing where to live. She enjoys New York City, and has often considered moving there. But she realizes that if she moved, she would lose virtually all of her carefully cultivated clients. Contrast this with the geographical opportunities available to someone pursuing a career in banking. Where the stockbroker will have to begin her business from scratch should she move, the banker can actually gain in both salary and position by moving. In some respects, Amanda has built herself a gilded cage.

THE EXECUTIVE AS A HIRED HAND   Many assume that this lack of freedom is a temporary situation and that as they progress toward upper management, things will change. They believe that once they become a corporate "honcho," these restrictions will vanish.

Unfortunately, perquisites and lifestyle aside, the corporate executive is a "hired hand." He or she has no inherent freedoms—only those that are granted by the organization. The typical executive is locked into the job and chained to the company. He must work 9-to-5 every day, forty-eight weeks or so out of the year. He can't take off for a two month sail through the Caribbean on his boat, even though he can afford it financially. In fact, he may find it difficult to plan even a three week trip, as his superiors would consider it irresponsible to be incommunicado for such a long period of time.

Consider the right to control one's destiny when it comes to the company transfer. Most personnel executives agree that a professional can only turn down a transfer once or possibly twice without incurring permanent career damage. Thus, executives, if they wish to maintain their upward momentum in an organization, move when and where the company directs. Even if it means a spouse must quit his or her job and that they must take their children out of school in mid-season.

This situation changes very little the higher one goes. Usually, the more important the job, the less freedom that accompanies it. With every promotion in the organization, one's actions are delineated more specifically: drive a certain class of car, belong to a specific club, or live in a particular geographical area of town.

4

THE FACTS OF LIFE

Debunking the myths about business

THERE ARE probably more myths, preconceptions, and misunderstandings about business and how it works than about any other kind of career, with the possible exception of medicine. We live in an era when business in general, and management in particular, is glorified. The corporate world has taken on an almost mythical facade—where fortunes are made and superstars wage power battles on a larger-than-life scale. While this translates well into movies and fiction, the reality, with occasional notable exceptions, is not nearly as exciting or as grand.

Adding to this distorted image of the business world is the fact that many pursuing business careers today have been inundated with advice which often serves only to perpetuate these myths. Many business school graduates, for example (unlike those of a generation ago), expect their work to offer intellectual stimulation, challenge, excitement, friendship, and satisfaction.

They believe and expect that their jobs will enhance every aspect of their professional and personal lives. When their careers inevitably fail to meet these unrealistic expectations, they become disillusioned and confused. And they feel that they have somehow failed the job, rather than the reverse.

"THE PERFECT JOB" AND OTHER MYTHS

Attempting to make their jobs meet these lofty standards, they search for ways to accelerate their advancement, believing that the "perfect" job does exist—only it is at the next level, or at another company, or perhaps in another industry.

In previous generations, businessmen and women often stayed with one company throughout an entire career. But it is a fact of contemporary corporate life that most people entering business in the last decade or so will change companies at least several times. While many will attribute their job changes to a better title, a bigger salary, or more responsibility, often the real reason is that they are still searching for that Holy Grail, the perfect job.

Many fall victim to this perfect job myth. Others may envelop themselves in their career, hoping naively that extra long work and company loyalty will be rewarded. For others, "mentor" has replaced the knight in shining armor of yesteryear, and networking—the modern day version of the "coffee klatch"—is thought to offer up the key to rapid advancement.

THE SEVEN MOST PREVALENT MYTHS
ABOUT BUSINESS

MYTH 1
Business is fair

Victims of this myth believe that if you work hard, you will be rewarded with promotions. If your work has merit, the company will see its value. If you are loyal to the company, the company will be loyal to you. Finally, if you are fair with your boss and your business associates they will be the same with you.

THE REALITY

This widely held belief about the fairness of business probably evolved from the American educational system, and is based upon the belief of many that the so-called "Protestant work" ethic will be rewarded.

· Hard work in and of itself is rarely rewarded. And while a company will exact as much work as possible from each employee, it doesn't often promote individuals solely on the basis of hard work.

· Quality is a highly subjective term, and the way your work is received by management is more dependent upon politics and your image than its true value.

· Loyalty on the part of the company lasts only as long as it serves the company's purposes. If you are undergoing personal problems, you will keep your job as long as your difficulties don't affect your work. Once they do, the company will quickly forget your years of faithful service, and you'll be gone.

· The maxim of "fair play" does not prevail in most business organizations. If a colleague can get credit for your idea, he or she will. And if it will increase the chances of getting a promotion, your business associate will find a way to let management know of your weaknesses.

Most companies care little for their employees on an individual basis. Any action on their part which appears to indicate otherwise can always be shown as ultimately good for the company. As disappointing as it may be, fairness simply doesn't have a place in the lexicon of American business.

MYTH 2
Networking is a valued success strategy for women

Networking is a popular success theory based on the "old boy network," an age-old strategy for men.

Networking is supposed to assist participants in acquiring jobs at other companies, provide useful tips and strategies for succeeding, and serve as the basis for functional power and political alliances.

Networks for women are theoretically composed of individuals in different levels of organizations. These women are united by a common bond of being female in business. They meet in some regular fashion to share their experiences and to lend a helping hand to their fellow "networkers."

If the "old boy network" works, why doesn't the "old girl network"?

There is a basic element missing from the embryonic old girl network that is intrinsic to the all-male alliance. The men's network has the advantage of power at the top of organizations.

- Contact with senior level people, whether personally or as part of an organization, is a great asset in business. For a network to be successful it must have such people, not just to provide access to specific jobs, but to offer meaningful direction and insight. Most women's networks suffer from a paucity of top echelon women. The result is a group of mostly low level women who are in no position to help someone else get ahead.
- Many networks are havens for women who are insecure about themselves and their jobs, and want the security of a group. Women in these groups end up exchanging emotional support with women who are in identical predicaments. While there is nothing wrong with this, it hardly serves as a positive tool for the ambitious professional.
- Networks are touted as opportunities to get "a foot in the door" of another company. Some middle-management women even cite instances of young networking acquaintances demanding that they set up a job interview for them. No woman executive who meets you on such a casual basis is going to put her credibility on the line by recommending you. There are faster and more reliable ways to secure an interview with a company.

Rarely will these groups result in any real positive advancement for your career. If you wish to join one, you must see the women's network as an innocuous social activity.

MYTH 3
Hard work pays off with success

Hard work pays off. There is simply no better way to succeed than by working long hours, producing more than everyone else, and maintaining high quality. There is a direct and positive correlation between work and success within a company.

We wouldn't be surprised if this myth were perpetuated by companies wanting more work from their employees, without having to pay more money. It is also related to the "Business is fair" myth. The reality is that there is no direct correlation between hard work and success.

- Hard work can actually hinder your career progress. A recent study of successful executives indicated that they usually devote 50 percent of their working hours to paperwork and 50 percent on "self-promotion" and politics. The hard working professional who lunches at the desk, passes up after-work socializing with colleagues, and forgoes company outings to do more work is ignoring the social and political nature of a professional management position.
- Another survey, conducted by the *Wall Street Journal,* indicated that 83 percent of the top executives who lost their jobs showed a common trait. They depended on their good work to speak for itself, and didn't expend sufficient effort to bring it to their superior's attention.
- Another negative effect is that people who focus on output sometimes doom themselves to their current position. Their canny superiors don't want to lose that productivity to someone else by promoting them. (Women are more susceptible to this trap than men, often killing their career by becoming "indispensable" in a certain area.)

We are not saying that substantial work output, in quality and quantity, is not positive. Merely that working hard is just one of the many attributes and qualities necessary for long-term success in management.

MYTH 4
Somewhere, there is the perfect job for me

There is a "perfect" position for you. It's out there somewhere. If you only had it, you would not have any of the problems you have with your current job. You would be challenged, excited, and fascinated by every aspect of the position—and your performance would shine. In fact, you are convinced that most of your career difficulties can be traced to the fact that you haven't found that perfect job, yet. Your beliefs are confirmed when you consider other people's jobs, which always seem to be better than your own.

THE REALITY

The perfect job. It simply doesn't exist. You can't find it, and no one else has it.

· Envying another person's job is natural. From the outside, many jobs seem to offer exactly what your position lacks. But these perfect jobs exist only in the observer's imagination. Don't expect the people in these supposedly enviable positions to expose the "grit beneath the glitter" of their jobs. Everyone has a vested interest in acting as if he or she does indeed have an ideal job. (In reality, your envy may be the only good thing about their job.)

· No job is without drawbacks. People who continue to believe in the existence of the perfect job will end up frustrated and bitter, in much the same manner as those who continue to search for the perfect mate, disdaining those with even minor flaws. The perfect job seekers will have gone from one job to another in rapid succession, always feeling that somehow they missed the "golden" opportunity.

We are not saying that some jobs aren't better than others. Clearly, some are far superior. It's just that every job, whether in the executive suite or the mail room, comes with its rewards and drawbacks.

MYTH 5
Women and bonding

As the "new kids on the block" in the business world, women know they are a minority and that many barriers against their advancement still exist. For that reason, women within the same company will bond together to overcome these obstacles. They will empathize with each other, and help each other.

If only wishing would make it true! Often, exactly the opposite occurs. Rather than see each other as allies, many women view other women in their organization as a greater threat to their careers than their male colleagues.

- As surprising as it may seem, there is generally little "bonding" among minorities at a company. Many minority members are convinced that there are a limited number of spots in the organization that are really available to them. They may believe, for example, that for every ten existing middle-manager positions, only two or three will be filled by minorities. As a result, there is a perception of greater competition with other minority members in the organization than with mainstream white males, who represent the preponderance of professionals in the management ranks of American industry.
- Many minority members enjoy their unique status in the white, male-dominated business establishment. They often, justifiably, see their uniqueness as accelerating their upward mobility. Some will feel threatened by another minority of the same group who will dilute that visibility.

Two women at the same level in an organization are more likely to view one another as direct competitors than to see each other as allies in the "grand feminist struggle." Experience with other minority groups in business seems to uphold this somewhat pessimistic point. On the other hand, it should not be so surprising that such a situation occurs. After all, it is merely human nature to enjoy the spotlight and the attention of others. And it is only natural that one would not wish to lose that visibility. Even brothers and sisters in the same family vie with one another for attention of their parents. Why should we expect that women in business are any different from the rest of humanity?

MYTH 6
Women will humanize business

Business is often guilty of less than altruistic behavior. Companies may be aloof and sometimes callous to employees, bosses may usurp credit for subordinates' work, and colleagues may engage in vicious back-stabbing. But this will abate with the influx of women into the business world.

With their innate nurturing and caring qualities, women will "humanize" business as they ascend the corporate hierarchy. They will discard the existing negative male characteristics. Rather than be changed by the business world, women will change it.

Even if one lends credence to the so-called natural differences between the sexes, it takes a rather significant leap in logic to assume that women will change the nature of business. And mounting evidence appears to contradict the theory.

- One problem with this idea is that it ignores the rite of passage to the top of a business organization. Since men are still in positions of power, the women who will be successful are those who are able to assimilate that culture. In other words, those women who can closely match the characteristics of those in power. In order to survive and flourish, women must adapt to the pre-existing business world.
- Many of the so-called traditional values of women have been thrust upon them by society. There is simply no precedence to predict what will happen when they are left to choose their own values.

These so-called "nurturing traits" are not being exhibited by successful female managers. As we noted in the first chapter, a recent study found that women who are progressing in corporate America are not bringing these presumed feminine traits to their positions. Instead, they are exhibiting those attitudes normally attributed to men.

MYTH 7
Mentoring plays a key role in women's business sucess

The mentor myth espouses the idea that women in business need a mentor to succeed in the business world. A mentor is defined as someone with power at least a few levels above the protégé who serves as a "guide" through the complexities of the organization.

The idea is derived from the fact that some men in the business world have been helped immensely by mentors. Utilizing the old adage that "what is good for the goose is good for the gander," many books and business articles today tout the positive effects of seeking and cultivating a mentor.

There are success stories of younger men who have been mentored by older, more powerful men. But this is not as common an occurrence as is portrayed. More to the point, it doesn't always work, even for men. In reality, mentoring is a double-edged sword.

- A study conducted by the National Science Foundation determined that of 3,000 mentor-protégé pairs, only 34 lasted three years or more without a fight terminating the relationship. Further, more than 1,200, or 40 percent, of the protégés reported being fired by their mentors.
- One pitfall is choosing the wrong person to cultivate as your guide. For a mentor to be of real value, he or she should be fairly high up in management. But it is difficult to assess the politics in an organization more than a level or two above your own. You may very easily, through lack of knowledge, select a mentor who is on the way out. And with the mentor's departure, you could find yourself on the losing side of a political conflict.
- Resentment from others is another serious drawback. No one will be thrilled with the idea that you have a powerful mentor. Your colleagues will be jealous, and your boss will be antagonized. And they would all enjoy seeing you knocked down from your protected position.
- For women, the situation is fraught with even greater drawbacks. A professional woman can rarely enter into a mentor relationship with a man (and let's face it, most mentors will be male given the scarcity of women in positions of power) without inciting innuendo. At a minimum, you will be the focus of damaging speculative gossip.
- For some, the mentoring relationship does drift toward a sexual relationship. Attribute it up to the natural at-

traction of the sexes, or to the stimulating effects of power (his) and dependency (yours). As Henry Kissinger once noted, "Power is the greatest aphrodisiac." If you go along with this tendency, you are playing with dynamite; if you resist it, you risk destroying your relationship in short order.

A final irony is that many lose sight of the proverbial "forest for the trees." Some women get so caught up in looking for an easy way of succeeding (via mentoring) that they lose track of more important success strategies. Others, when they fail to find or keep that powerful ally on whom they have pinned their career hopes, feel doomed to failure.

5

PASSAGES

Phases of a successful career

I N THE 1960S BROADWAY MUSICAL "How to Succeed in Business Without Really Trying," young J. Pierpont Finch had a problem. It was his first day in the corporate mail room, and he discovered that his boss had waited twenty-five years to be promoted. But J. Pierpont didn't want to be stuck in the mail room for a quarter of a century. So he decided to accelerate his career. Through a combination of bold risk-taking, cleverness, and scheming that would make a Harvard MBA green with envy, he climbed the corporate ladder swiftly. In a short time, he was being groomed for the presidency of the firm.

Unfortunately, this was just a play. In real life, one quickly learns that there really aren't that many shortcuts to the top.

CORPORATE PASSAGES

Just as Gail Sheehey chronicled predictable stages in life in her classic book *Passages*, it is possible to demarcate various phases of a career. Not everyone will pass through each phase. Some will skip a phase through luck, being in the right place at the right time, or by virtue of family connections. Others will only progress to a certain point and go no further. But most careers will tend to fit the pattern, and each phase brings with it specific crises and obstacles. To be successful long term, it naturally follows that you must be successful in each phase.

While we like to think of ourselves as unique, it is clear

that people in management careers tend to follow patterns. But many people fail to realize this and are destined to repeat the mistakes of others. Understanding these phases will shed light on your career and make it easier to cope with and flourish within the system.

In speaking of careers, we're referring to professional business careers. It is generally only in these careers that one can expect to advance up the "ladder." This progress takes the form of significant promotions and salary increases. Since marked advancement via promotion in other nonprofessional jobs is unusual, the concept of phasing doesn't apply.

The key concept of career phasing is that every phase has specific requirements for success. Actions and style that generate positive response in one stage may not engender the same results in another. The requisites for growth and change can be quite challenging, and many career crises can be traced to a failure to meet the conditions of a certain phase. For any success strategy to be worthwhile, it must be relevant to each phase.

THE PROTO CAREER PHASE: THE INTERNSHIP

Those in this pre-career phase hold quasi-professional positions. These jobs are occupied by college students in their junior or senior years or graduate business school students between their first and second years. While there are a variety of positions that fall into the category of intern, such as those in publicity, publishing, and government, we are focusing on those positions offered by major corporations in fields such as marketing, finance, and consulting.

While some internships offer no salary, it is not unusual for interns to be paid substantial sums. Outrageous may be a more appropriate term if you have been privy to the work requirements of an intern. (Summer MBA interns at the Boston Consulting Group earn approximately $1,200 per week.) And despite their apparently limited, low-level position, they often have high visibility within the company. Many, in fact, are encouraged to have contact with senior-level management in seeming violation of the chain of command cultural factor.

Special privileges of the intern

Firms using internship positions are rewarded for their efforts. By hiring business school students during their interim summer, they get a year's jump on competitors for top MBA graduates. When the intern returns to school, the company benefits from the invaluable "word of mouth" publicity.

For these reasons, many companies lavish special attention on interns. Interns are usually paid far more than their limited experience and maturity warrant (certainly more than their actual contributions would indicate), and their egos are "stroked" regularly. The work that they are assigned often has little relevance to the business (busywork), and is designed to be involving and stimulating for the intern, rather than to accomplish anything.

The intern phase, however, can be a double-edge sword. There will never be quite the same opportunity to cut through different levels of the organization with such ease. The visibility, courtship, and freedom of this phase will be sorely missed when the intern returns to take a true professional position.

Success strategies for the intern

The best approach is to view the internship as a twofold opportunity. First, consider it as an extended job interview. Use the freedom and flexibility to make a positive impression on management and to establish good contacts.

Second, use it as a learning experience. Don't restrict yourself to the specifics of the job. Explore the politics and inner workings of the company. Management often shows great patience with an intern—far more than is accorded to regular employees. And don't be afraid of making mistakes. Frankly, from the company's perspective, it is difficult for an intern to do any wrong.

At one prestigious company, Steve, a Harvard MBA intern, was well known for playing "basketball" for a good part of the day. The highly paid young intern alternated his day between tossing rolled up paper balls into the brand group's wastebasket and meeting with members of upper management. Despite this, he was not only invited to return to the company following his graduation, but he was offered an unusually high salary.

In fact, he was wooed so diligently that the only mitigating solace for the rest of the brand group was the day of reckoning—when Steve returned to the company after graduation as a member of the rank and file, and at the bottom!

THE NEOPHYTE PHASE

We've named the first true stage on the professional track the "Neophyte Phase." Typically, the person is a recent college or business school graduate, and the job is defined as "entry level" for professionals.

It is easy to differentiate between the intern and the neophyte stages. Interns are usually hired for a temporary period of time. Since no specific duties exist, projects are created for them. In the Neophyte Phase, the company hopes that the employee will fit in and stay for a long period of time. The neophyte has specific responsibilities to assume, and is on the first step on the route to upper management.

Great expectations of the neophyte

The neophyte position is usually held by people in their mid-to-late twenties. In this stage, the employee is typically naive and has many misconceptions about the true nature of business. The sky seems to be the limit for career dreams. Aspirations of being the youngest vice-president abound. The indoctrination of academia, in which work is usually quantifiable and graded accordingly, still exists. And the religion of "hard work and goodness reaping rewards" is fervently believed.

DREAMS DIE QUICKLY   But the crises involved in the Neophyte Phase can begin even before the first day on the job. Take the case of Anne, a recent college graduate. During the last six months of school, she went through many interviews on campus, and was invited for second interviews off campus. She received four job offers. The company she finally accepted had put her through no less than six interviews before making an offer to her.

Anne began work with great expectations. After a few weeks, however, this excitement turned to disappointment as she realized that her assignments were little more than clerical busywork. Anne had expected that she would be assigned heavyweight responsibilities, particularly after the emphasis her business courses placed on management strategies and problems.

This disillusionment often occurs when the neophyte has learned just enough about the business to realize that the projects are not that important. This realization usually hits during the first six months on the job. A further jolt to the ego comes upon discovering that every bit of work is double- or even triple-checked.

Reality shock

Ted, a top student at Stanford Business School, knew that he was "hot property." His educational background was impressive and his non-academic achievements were noteworthy. He exemplified the type of candidate that the best companies actively seek.

During the school's recruiting season, Ted was taken to the best restaurants in San Francisco and treated to all-expense paid trips to prospective company headquarters, including some on the East Coast. After meeting with executives from each company, Ted finally decided to join a prestigious marketing firm in New York City.

The company's enthusiasm for Ted was obvious, and he envisioned a fulfilling and challenging career. As confirmation, he was assigned to a high-priority brand group specializing in new product development. Then, Ted received his first assignment: to purchase toilet tissue, each brand and color stocked on the shelves of area grocery stores. Once he had representatives of all brand name and generic tissues, he was to tabulate by hand the number of sheets in each roll. His second project consisted of coloring a map indicating prospective test-market sites with crayons. Within a month, Ted had developed a strong case of "reality shock."

Both Anne and Ted encountered an all too common problem of the Neophyte Phase. Their education and the lavish attentions of corporate recruiters set them up for disappointment. The attention and ego gratification of being chosen via a rigorous selection process often raised their expectations far beyond reality.

Chomping at the bit (under 30)

Early disillusionment is just one of the problems characteristic of this phase. Anxiety about promotion is also a common concern, since there is no set timetable. The time spent as a neophyte is arbitrary and depends upon a number of factors. Job performance usually is not the most important determinant.

Consider Mark, a 27-year-old financial analyst in Boston. He has been in his current position for three years and hopes that he will soon be rewarded with a promotion to a position of "real responsibility" as department manager.

Career phasing is working against Mark. Most companies are controlled by people in their fifties who rarely view someone under 30 as capable of handling true responsibility. (When James Bere, the former chairman of Borg-Warner, became a group executive at the age of 41, he was still addressed by one of the divisional presidents as "kid.")

As a result, the most Mark can expect before he is 30 are ceremonial promotions, a senior analyst title for example, with little substantive change in responsibility from his entry-level position. In many cases, it is simply biological age, rather than length of service, which determines promotion time.

WHERE YOUTH REIGNS SUPREME   This under thirty discrimination phenomenon is widespread throughout most of the business world, with the exception of certain high-tech firms. Quite a few firms in the Silicon Valley micro-chip mecca have built mini-empires with neophytes. But a primary, and logical reason for this is the fact that the high-tech world is still in its infancy. Only the most recent college graduates are intimately familiar with high technology.

Apple Computer, Inc., was for a number of years a highly publicized example of youthful management. Stephen Jobs, the 29-year-old founder had surrounded himself with high-powered managers still in their mid-to-late twenties. But, interestingly, this situation came to an abrupt end in mid-1985 when Jobs was forced out of the active management of the company. Power was assumed by John Sculley, 45, the former PepsiCo executive Jobs himself had brought to Apple a year before.

RUNNING THE MARATHON   In other areas of business there is no fundamental disparity between the academic training of the last few years and that of 10 or 20 years ago. An accounting course taught 20 years ago is essentially the same as one taught last year. In most traditional industries, emphasis and value is placed upon those with both academic background and long-term experience.

No one in the upper echelons, then, really expects much of anyone under 30, including chest-thumping MBA "hot shots." Consequently, management rarely bestows major promotions on people in their twenties, regardless of their impressive credentials or performance. Accepting this is difficult for the ambitious individual at the beginning of a career. Success in business is more akin to a marathon, rather than a 100-meter sprint. The earlier you learn this lesson the better.

THE RITES OF PASSAGE   Once you learn the realities, this

can be a very productive time. Accept the limitations as a fact of business life, and use the neophyte stage to develop and perfect a personal success style.

Strengthen your basic business skills, observe the characteristics and styles that are rewarded by your company. Assess your competitive advantage. Reevaluate the appropriateness of your career selection and your company. If either feels wrong, this is the optimum time to change. Don't compete where the odds are against you. You can make a lateral career change at this point with little penalty.

PAYING YOUR DUES   The most damaging thing you can do in this phase is to become angry or bitter at your lack of an important role. Too often people feel that the company is ignoring them, or that management doesn't appreciate their work. Women are especially vulnerable to this disillusionment. After all, barriers to their advancement still exist in business, and the delays inherent in this phase can easily be perceived as just one more form of discrimination.

While prejudice against women does exist in some areas of business, it is important to distinguish it from the normal delays of the Neophyte Phase. (If anything, these are prejudices against youth.) This is a time-honored tradition called "paying one's dues." If you handle it with style, you will reap the rewards in your thirties, the Junior Management Phase.

THE JUNIOR MANAGEMENT PHASE

Transition to the Junior Management Phase is the first bottleneck to the top. It usually involves a quantum leap in responsibility from the neophyte level, and may be the second or third titular promotion in a career. Earlier promotions, within the Neophyte Phase, such as Mark's promotion to senior analyst, should not be confused with elevation to the next real level on the corporate ladder.

Promotion from the neophyte level usually comes when phasing, job performance, and other factors mesh. After four or five years, you should begin to notice that you are perceived, quite naturally and without any fanfare, as more mature and responsible. You look older, are taken more seriously by management, and receive projects which test and strengthen your managerial mettle. Your promotion to a true junior management level position probably will come shortly.

Comparison with the Neophyte Phase

Emphasis on style and skills changes from the Neophyte Phase. Your personal life usually becomes a more important factor in how the company perceives you. As a neophyte no one really cared how you spent your spare time. In the Junior Management Phase, however, your personal and social life begin to affect your professional image.

As a neophyte nobody expected you to advance quickly because you were seen as too young for real responsibility. You had more latitude for errors and politically imprudent actions. At the Junior Management Phase, however, the rules are more strict.

At this stage the grooming and culling-out process begins. You are constantly being evaluated and compared to the competition. It is a trial by fire ordeal. If you come through unscathed and in an acceptable time frame, you are headed for upper management.

Because there are so few spots at the top, however, candidates with weaknesses are usually eliminated at this level or relegated to non-line positions. It is survival of the most adaptive. Success in this phase does not indicate that one is more intelligent or talented. It merely signifies that through a combination of persistence, luck, competitive advantages, and personal power, the survivors avoided fatal pitfalls.

This phase is in many respects a watershed on the journey to top management. During this time, the junior manager should be looking for ways to create visibility with the important people, the decision makers, and to expand his or her field of expertise.

THE MIDDLE AND UPPER MANAGER PHASE

The next phase in a successful career is the Middle Management Phase. It begins for most people in their late thirties and early forties, although this varies from one industry to another. This is usually the beginning of true corporate responsibility. It also represents the highest level that many in the race to corporate stardom will ever achieve.

One way to distinguish between a true middle-management position and a junior-management position is to consider the nature of the leadership function, the manner of overall direction of subordinates, as well as the stability of the position. Junior managers, for example, rarely initiate action on their own, and take direction from above. Their positions are somewhat unstable.

In contrast, middle managers exercise true leadership. They set the major themes for their areas of responsibility, and they can personally determine the direction of their subordinates. Junior management, on the other hand, follows and implements these initiatives, usually under close supervision.

Middle managers share responsibility for the overall company and identify strongly with the organization. The typical middle manager is fairly well entrenched within the company and is considered a long-term prospect. The middle manager is often too financially involved via pension plans and other perks, and too psychologically committed, to consider changing companies except in unusual circumstances. Compare this to the Junior Management Phase, when job changes are frequent.

Middle management is the final test before admittance to upper management. As with each phase, you should assess objectively your chances of promotion within the company. If you stay too long and are not promoted, you will find it difficult to jump to a higher position in another company, having been tagged as "deadwood."

Making the "big move" is done frequently with great success by middle-level managers who recognized that their career in a company was stagnant. Before the stall became known in the industry, they moved to another company where they quickly made it into upper management. But such moves should be taken only when you have peaked at your current company, or when you seek career rewards that your company cannot meet.

Middle management career crises

The middle management stage is the time for the greatest career crises that most face. With few exceptions, the dreams of glory that the professional had in his or her early twenties will not be achieved. It becomes apparent that few are going to command enormous salaries or make the cover page of *Business Week* or *Forbes*. The forties are for many a time of disappointment, regret, and bitterness. The possibilities that seemed limitless at 20 appear all too limited at 40. Many will end their careers in this phase.

Confronted with the apparent end of youthful dreams, some managers react emotionally. They wrongly assume that because they haven't made it to the top in their company, their career is finished. They do not realize that they are merely passing through a psychological and emotional stage that many people have, or will, pass through. And in many cases, the people who have handled this period well have gone on to the top.

A well-known example of this is Ronald Reagan. At an age when most people are planning retirement, Reagan, who was considered a political has-been, initiated a comeback. Despite a failed try for the presidency in 1976, Reagan pressed on against the odds. And of course, he finally won the most prestigious of all "top spots." In addition, he made a successful and dramatic career change from acting to politics. (Although sometimes it is difficult to isolate the difference between these two professions.)

Others will have to realize that they will go no further

in their careers. For these people, it is time to look for satisfaction in other areas that they may have neglected as they pursued their careers. Far from being a time for failure, this can open up the possibilities of a more balanced and satisfying life.

Upper management

Finally we reach the pinnacle of the corporate career, upper management. Since this book is concerned mainly with those in the first phases of their career, we will not dwell here on the rewards, or the concomitant sacrifices, of life at the top. Nor will we explore the final phase of a career—the inevitable loss of power as those at the top must step aside for the next generation of managers.

THE IMPORTANCE OF CAREER PHASING

Why discuss "career passages" at all? And what relevance do they have to career success? Most of us are able to deal better with circumstances and resolve crises if we can anticipate situations and understand that others undergo similar experiences.

If you are out of step with your career phase because of age, personality, experience, or style—you are probably not going to be promoted. The 25-year-old businesswoman is rarely going to be elevated to junior management, regardless of her efforts. Her understanding that this is a normal phase of career development will soften much of the disillusionment that would otherwise result.

A junior executive may have difficulty being promoted to middle management if she does not exhibit signs of "settling" down. If she is still cultivating the lifestyle of a junior executive, it may be hard for people to see her as a middle manager. If you recognize that your personal life can have a dramatic effect at this career phase, you could assure your promotion into the next phase.

While career phasing is a definable phenomenon, you can

circumvent some of its obstacles once you realize what each phase entails. Take the case of the junior executive. To convey an impression of personal responsibility, the junior manager could buy a house or even consider marriage. It's no coincidence that many men get married at the same time that their company is searching for people who project stability in both their personal and professional life.

Coping with career phasing

Understanding phasing helps one to understand the increasingly restrictive set of expectations that are imposed upon a professional as he or she passes through the Junior Management and Middle Management phases.

In the Neophyte Phase, for example, an active social life is not only accepted but expected. During the latter part of the junior management stage, however, it can have a negative impact. Consider how youthful exuberance and enthusiasm are qualities often indicative of a neophyte, whereas reserve and polish is expected from a junior executive.

In his early years at General Motors, John DeLorean offered the precise profile that the company was looking for in its junior- and middle-level managers. He was of lower-middle-class origins, attended a small technical college, and did not have a graduate business degree. He accepted the establishment at GM, was described as the "squarest guy in the world" by an associate, and married a secretary at the company. At 32, he was becoming too flabby to fit into his suits (all three of them). In short, his behavior fit the company's phasing expectations and requirements, and he was promoted rapidly.

When he reached upper management, DeLorean decided to change his life. He lost weight, worked out, and divorced his then middle-aged wife. He dyed his hair and had a face-lift. He dated young models and starlets, traveling in the social "fast lane." This behavior, while it contributed to his ultimate departure from General Motors, did not have nearly the same effect it would have had if he had undergone this metamorphosis in his junior- or middle-management stages. As an upper-level manager, he was firmly entrenched and it was difficult to get rid of him. If he had changed his behavior earlier, without benefit of this power base, it probably would have been fatal for his career at General Motors.

Part Two

BASIC TACTICS

6

CORPORATE PRELIMS:

Choosing a job and a career

WHEN A JOB CANDIDATE is being recruited by Morgan Stanley, a prestigious New York investment banking firm, a key part of the interviewing process is dinner. The candidate and spouse are invited to dine with one of the firm's managing directors and his wife. During the meal, the director takes an unusual tack for a recruiter. Rather than conjure up a positive and irresistible picture of life at the investment house, he specifically points out the negatives of a career there. The recruit is told of the long and tedious work hours, personal sacrifices, exhausting business travel, and the demanding step-by-step climb to the top.

This image is often the antithesis of the high living, fast track, jet-set existence that the ambitious MBA has envisioned at Morgan Stanley. Many then opt for a different position in another company or even in another industry. Surprisingly, this is the result that the firm seeks.

As one of the most successful and well-managed investment banking houses, Morgan Stanley has a strong culture and a well-defined sense of what it takes to succeed there. The firm realizes the importance of an employee fitting in with the corporate culture, and puts great emphasis on that match from the beginning. They are not looking for individuals with a distorted or unrealistic concept of investment banking. Nor do they want people who will be out of sync or unhappy. In their experience, they have found that people who have a good grasp on the negatives of the position are more likely to succeed.

Unfortunately, Morgan Stanley's perceptive approach to interviewing is the exception rather than the rule. Many personnel recruiters take the opposite approach and attempt to paint a glittering facade on their organizations. They will do and say anything to entice a choice candidate into selecting their company. This is a short-sighted approach. In the long run, both the employee and the organization benefit if the employee understands the requirements for success in that company.

Choosing a career should entail more than becoming a consultant because it's the new "in" career for hot-shot MBAs; and selecting a company should involve more than simply going with the highest bidder. Yet many people make long-term decisions for these and other short-term reasons. Careers and companies are often chosen on a random, emotional, or even a casual basis rather than through practical analysis. And inevitably—sometimes early, sometimes late—reality intrudes, often with unpleasant results.

SELECTING A CAREER

A recent study conducted by John Crystal, president of John C. Crystal, Inc., a New York career-counsulting firm, concluded that 80 percent of working Americans are in the "wrong" job. Fifty-two percent of the executives reported their jobs to be unsatisfying. If researched further, it would most likely be found that a major reason for dissatisfaction was a fundamental mismatch of person and job. This unhappy situation can be avoided or at least ameliorated by putting more thought into selecting a career.

John Noble, associate director of Harvard University's Office of Career Development, recommends starting with a frank self-appraisal. "List your talents and skills in one column and your weaknesses in another. Be realistic. For example, while most people like to think that they get along well with people, or that they like people, few have really nurtured this trait to the point where it can be of special value in business."

Women in particular often tout this as one of their strengths during interviews. If you do indeed have a special talent for dealing with and motivating others, list it. If, however, your admiration of this trait leads you to believe you have it, don't list it. And if you actually have a difficult time motivating people, put it under your weakness column.

Noble suggests some personal characteristics that you should consider:

· People skills
· Analytical skills
· Writing skills
· Oral communication skills
· Energy level
· Ability to conform
· Need for variety in daily work
· Work location preference: in or out of the office
· Amount of travel
· What type of business attracts you?
· Degree of self-initiative
· Geographical requirements and degree of flexibility regarding later moves

Your strengths and weaknesses may not be immediately apparent. If you have not yet worked in a professional capacity, evaluate your previous experiences both in and out of school to determine your talents and inclinations. Internship positions are invaluable in making your assessment.

Matching reward factors and corporate cultures

Ultimately you will be most satisfied and fulfilled if you receive the career rewards that are meaningful for you. If your prime motivation for working is to amass a small fortune, then you should look for a specific career that makes that goal realistic, and not be sidetracked by status or glamour.

Look for cultural patterns that suit you best. If you have a relaxed style and prefer to make decisions in a thoughtful, calm atmosphere, then clearly a high pressure, "seat of the pants" type industry, such as securities trading, is not for you.

Playing to your "competitive advantage"

Skill and talent do not guarantee success. (How often have you heard of someone considered very talented and intelligent who just couldn't make it in business?) Business laurels go to those who play to their "competitive advantage."

What is a competitive advantage? Simply, it is something that gives you an edge over others in a job. If you were an athlete with powerful shoulder and arm muscles, you would have an advantage over others if you chose to compete as a swimmer. Yet, these same muscles would be of little benefit if you chose to be a sprinter.

The same prevails in business. If you work in sales and possess a way of making people open up to you immediately, you have a competitive advantage in the field. But these same talents would only be moderate strengths for an accountant. It is not the talent or style per se which establishes the advantage—it is the match of both with the environment.

Choosing a career and a company in which your particular talent, ability, and style will be appreciated and rewarded, maximizes your chances for success. Before starting your career "marathon," it pays to put some thought to the race you are best suited to "run."

Lifestyle fit

Consider the lifestyle you're planning, and select a career that enables you to fulfill it. If you want to combine work and family life, for example, look for a career that will allow you a reasonable amount of personal time. For example, careers in banking, finance, and sales follow fairly standard work weeks.

On the other hand, if you choose a career such as consulting or investment banking, you could constantly be torn between your career and personal life. Consultants, especially those in the major firms, work far more than the standard eight-hour day and spend a great deal of time traveling. And investment bankers can become immersed in twenty-hour work days. Such schedules do not offer much time for a family.

Once you have determined your strengths and weaknesses, your career expectations, and your fit requirements, review those opportunities that offer the best chance of achieving your goals. Don't make the mistake of feeling that you must have altruistic motives in selecting a career. A typical example of this is the oft-cited goal of wanting to "help people." You won't help yourself or anybody else if you select a career because you think it's the "right" thing to do.

SELECTING A COMPANY

You are completing college or graduate business school, or perhaps you are unhappy with your job, and feel that you would be better off in another firm. What should your key considerations be in selecting a company?

First, consider companies which emphasize your particular professional interests. If you are a financial analyst, then investigate companies where finance holds the spotlight. A financial analyst position at ITT, a strong financially oriented organization, would make more career sense than a similar position at General Foods, where marketing management holds all the attention.

Resume companies

In every industry there are companies considered "the best" at what they do. They are also highly regarded for the training of their employees. Typically, these companies hire a large number of new recruits every year from colleges and business schools, and place them in entry-level training programs.

For many, this training will be useful throughout a career. There is simply no equivalent for learning how the best outfits function. And as if that weren't enough, these companies also offer another invaluable benefit. A strong resume effect.

Consider the computer industry. There are many companies, particularly smaller ones, that could provide a good initial experience in the industry. But starting at IBM, even if you find some of its uniformity and rigidity unappealing, may be well worth it. Not only will you have a solid base of training and experience, but you will carry an impressive, widely admired credential on your resume throughout your career. (A personnel executive at Coca-Cola, regarding their hiring policies, remarked that, "You could say that we are looking for the IBM type—very professional, the crème de la crème." In fact, a number of ex-IBM managers now work at Coke.)

Our suggestion is to consider a "resume company," even if it does not provide the best fit on other considerations. This may seem to contradict some of our other advice, but we see this as one permissible exception. Consider starting at a resume company in your chosen field, even if the organization's style, location, or salary doesn't precisely meet your needs. Since most people spend only a few years at their first company, it should be well worth the investment.

The list on the following page gives examples of some training/resume companies by industry. We are not saying that these companies are better than others, or that you will have a better experience at them. We are merely suggesting that because of the way they are perceived, they have long-term career enhancing value.

Management development plans

Ask your prospective company about its programs for spotting managerial talent and developing it properly. Many companies are becoming aware of the importance of not only getting good people, but keeping and moving them upward.

Resume companies by industry*

Sales:	IBM, Procter & Gamble
Computers:	IBM
Investment Banking:	Morgan Stanley, Goldman Sachs
Banking:	Citibank, Morgan Guaranty
Stockbrokerage:	Merrill Lynch
Advertising:	Ogilvy & Mather; Young & Rubicam
Accounting Firms:	Any of the Big Eight
Consulting:	McKinsey & Company, Bain & Company
Retailing:	Federated Department Stores, Neiman Marcus
Brand Management:	Procter & Gamble
Electronics/Appliances:	General Electric
Chemicals:	Dupont
Oil:	Shell, Exxon

*This is meant only as a representative list; there are many other companies and industries which would fit our criteria.

They are implementing formalized "Management-Succession" planning programs. These programs provide a better chance of receiving good training, exposure to a variety of tasks, and a shot at a top spot in the company. And while these programs may not always work as they're supposed to, they indicate a progressive, professionally run organization. Some organizations that utilize this approach are Citibank, General Electric, Pillsbury, IBM, Exxon, Rockwell International, and Hewlett-Packard.

Line of business

Some prospective employer's products may be innately more appealing to you, and on this basis you might assume that you would be happy in that company. For example, you may be attracted to scientific or medical products. Or fashion and design may hold your interest. While we don't want to discount the relevance of working for a firm that is involved with products that are appealing to you, it is important to realize that "business is business," regardless of the specific product line involved.

Attraction to a company because of the nature of its activities is insufficient grounds to choose it. (The responsibilities of a sales manager handling consumer products is really no different from those dealing with office equipment.) Of much greater significance to your success are the "fit" factors that are derived from the business and the company's culture. After a short time on the job, the nature of your company's products will become a minor factor in determining whether you are happy and successful there.

Other considerations

Before selecting a company or an industry, consider the economic health of both. A company or industry encountering financial hard times, due to factors such as an eroding market share or increasing foreign competition, would probably not be the best choice. It would require an unusually satisfying and rewarding position to offset an atmosphere of low morale, shaky tenure, or stringent penny-pinching.

COMMON JOB TRAPS

During your search you may be tempted by positions which appear attractive on the surface, but in reality are fraught with pitfalls. While anyone can fall victim to these job traps, those starting out on their careers are especially vulnerable.

The impressive title

This position has an impressive title but little substance. While some industries, such as banking, suffer from innocuous title proliferation, the impressive title trap is an entirely different phenomenon. An example is a position with the title "Director of . . ." but the job is out in organizational left field with no clear-cut career path leading from it. In every sense other than the title, it's a dead-end position.

Quite often companies offer this type of position to women in order to demonstrate to the outside world that they are giving women greater responsibility. In actual fact, they are simply playing name games. It is difficult to go anywhere with this type of job.

Status

In the status trap, you accept a job because the company is currently in vogue—even if your position is unrelated to the company's mainstream business. During the heyday of Fred Silverman at ABC, many MBAs specializing in finance sought financial positions there to share in the excitement. Working for any of the networks at that time was considered so chic that even graduates of prestigious business schools accepted much lower salaries than their counterparts in less "glamourous" industries.

Suffice it to say that a financial analyst in an entertainment company never gets near the real action. Programming is the pulse of these companies. The financial analysts who were lured by the company's image ended up with low salaries and their noses pressed against the window of the programming department. Their careers would have been far better served if they had joined a company that focused primarily on finance.

The flashy job

Victims are lured by the "flash" or "glitter" of a job but career-wise there is no substance. The job may offer perks such as travel to exciting places or meeting famous and powerful people. Or, it could involve working with large sums of money. (Yes, to some that would be heaven on earth.) Obviously, these can add spice to any job, but if you are serious about your career you need to consider other aspects of the position.

Another twist to the flashy job trap is the misperception that those in lower-level positions bask in the reflected glory of those at the top. The presence of glamour at the top of an organization does not imply that it pervades the lower levels, even on a smaller scale.

Yet many people sought positions at the Chase Manhattan Bank in the 1970s because David Rockefeller headed it, just as many students wanted to attend Princeton University in the 1950s because Albert Einstein was on the faculty. At both institutions, the effect of the national repute of these men on the average individual was minimal.

The real challenge

A common trap for job seekers is a company which offers a "real challenge," "immediate responsibility," and a fast track to the top. This ploy is favored by smaller companies, where promises of high visibility sound plausible because there are so few people competing with you. The promises are often irresistible.

Few companies, large or small, give important responsibilities to new people, especially professionals fresh out of school. Everyone must earn their "stripes" with time, regardless of their talent and educational credentials. At most smaller companies, power is firmly entrenched in the hands of a few key people. This makes it all the more difficult to gain true responsibility.

If you are promised more than seems normal or reasonable for your background and experience, then look beneath the surface. Things probably are not what they seem. As the old saying goes, "If it seems too good to be true, it probably is."

7

INTERVIEWING

Getting the job you want

S o, TELL ME, why do they make man-hole covers round?"
The tall and intimidating partner at the prestigious
McKinsey & Company posed the question to the young
woman interviewing for a consulting position. She had prepared for and rehearsed over a hundred typical interview
questions, but she hadn't anticipated this one. She looked at
him suspiciously, but no, he wasn't joking. She realized that
if she couldn't give him the right answer she would probably
not get the job. So in the end, her education and hard work
all pivoted on one question.

She paused and then answered. A hint of satisfaction appeared on the interviewer's face. And the woman knew she
had the job.*

MAKING THE GRADE

Getting a job is not easy today, regardless of your background. Every year IBM interviews over 50,000 people for
6,000 slots. General Electric talks with 24,000 candidates to
fill just 2,000 openings. As John Noble, associate director of
Harvard University's Office of Career Development notes,
"With the increased competition for jobs today, and the current allure of professional careers, strong credentials alone
no longer insure anyone a suitable position. While the interview was always an important part of getting a job, it's even

* Answer at end of chapter.

more critical today." Since so many well-educated people are vying for too few positions, the interview is often the deciding factor in securing a job.

When viewed from the proper perspective, the interview game is easy to understand—and to manipulate to your advantage. Yet many people face it with considerable trepidation, and in doing so subconsciously shift the power balance in favor of the interviewer.

A *two-way street*

Both participants are under pressure. You, as a candidate, want to get a job offer. The interviewer also has a purpose—to sell his organization. He wants (and needs) to bring good people to the company. If he fails, management may think he cannot spot talent and he'll be replaced.

Many people forget this, become convinced that the interviewer is omnipotent, and are at a disadvantage. Under these circumstances the balance of power is tipped in favor of the recruiter.

DEVELOPING A HIRING PLAN

Before interviewing with potential employers, plan your career path. According to Dr. Roderick Hodgins, former director of placement at Harvard Business School, "You would be surprised at how many otherwise bright people don't know what direction they want to go in. That's why many business schools encourage their students to develop five- or even ten-year career plans." While few people adhere closely to their projected path, it does help to solidify career goals.

Resume *"waves"*

Once you have focused on a specific industry, list your top 10 or 15 company choices in order of preference. Divide the list in thirds. Send your first wave of letters to those that interest you least. Work your way up the list, saving your top third company choices for the last wave.

The reason for this staggered approach is simple. Generally, the first companies to receive your resume will be the first to invite you for an interview. You need to be comfortable with the interview situation, which necessitates practice. Polish your presentation with employers that are least important to you. This suggestion applies whether you are just beginning your career or changing companies.

Some feel that this approach is a waste of time for you and the interviewer. This opinion is usually voiced by recruiters or placement office supervisors who are trying to cut down on "frivolous" interviews. But they have their interests, not yours, at heart. No savvy person interviews at a first choice company without rehearsing. And no practice equals an actual interview. So put aside concerns for the recruiter's time and interview with a number of companies in your intended field.

You will undoubtedly receive feedback about your resume during your initial interviews. If it is useful, revise your resume. Sending your resume in staggered waves allows for revisions if necessary.

Sending the resume

Harvard's Noble also recommends forwarding a resume directly to the head of the department that interests you or to a higher level manager in the division. Use the personnel office only as a last resort. They are adequate for clerical workers and administrative people, but managerial candidates should avoid them. Although personnel people voice strong claims to the contrary, their department is often left isolated from management hiring needs. They are frequently unaware of professional openings until after they have been filled.

Even if personnel does play an active role in hiring, you will increase your chances of getting an interview by sending your resume directly to the specific department or division. The vice-president or department manager may receive only a handful of resumes a month. Thus yours has a better chance of standing out and generating positive action. Personnel, on the contrary, is often inundated with resumes for positions in every section of the company.

Cover letters

Some people recommend focusing on the "cover letter," which accompanies your resume. These letters are supposed to explain why you should be considered for the job, any special talents you may have, and your interest in the company. In reality, it makes more sense to concentrate on the resume itself. Keep the cover letter brief and to the point, unless you have some relevant information that would be inappropriate in the resume.

You will be considered for a job interview based upon your resume. No amount of superfluous personal hype in your cover letter is going to make much of a difference, and it could make you look foolish if you take the wrong approach. According to Deborah Brayton, former recruiting coordinator at Bain & Company, the Boston-based strategic consulting firm: "We considered people for interviews on the basis of their resumes, on their ability to put their background down concisely on one, at most two pages. Lengthy cover letters detract from this, are often repetitive, and rarely say anything of interest."

PREPARING FOR THE INTERVIEW

A common criticism of personnel managers is that many candidates don't really bother to prepare for an interview with a specific company. According to Harvard's John Noble, "Too often people seeking jobs expend all of their efforts in lining up interviews, and forget to prepare for them once they get them." While it is easy to fall into this trap (especially if you have many interviews scheduled), such nonchalance could destroy your chances for any offers. Preparation is the key to a successful interview.

You would not enter a battle unarmed against an armed

opponent. Going into an interview without strong preparation is just as foolish. Many companies now are putting their management-level personnel recruiters through intensive interview training programs. Shouldn't you do the same for yourself?

Getting the "scoop"

Know your prospective company. Go to the library and examine its annual reports, 10-K's, proxy statements, prospecta, and newspaper and magazine stories. Review back copies of the *Wall Street Journal* for recent activities of the company and the industry.

Get the "scoop" on the company through friends and acquaintances, or talk with someone who already works or has worked there. Use alumni office lists at your business school for additional contacts. However, avoid getting in touch with individuals who currently work in the anticipated department. They may reveal information about you to their managers that you would prefer they not know.

Stock questions

The range of potential interview questions might seem too extensive to anticipate. To a certain extent, that's true. Theoretically there is nothing, except common courtesy and a few laws, to keep the interviewer from asking anything that comes to mind. In actual fact, however, the same questions arise repeatedly, some so often that professional recruiters call them "stock questions."

Before your first interview, compile a list of such standard questions. Think about your answers, but don't memorize your responses or you'll risk coming across as stilted. Being unprepared for these predictable questions, which often constitute the bulk of most initial interviews, is foolish.

Some typical stock questions that everyone should be prepared for are:

· What do you know about our firm?
· What are your strengths?

- Your weaknesses?
- Where do you want to be five years from now?
- What other companies are you interviewing with?
- Give me an example of a time when you demonstrated leadership.
- Why do you want to work for our company?
- Have you ever worked for an incompetent boss?
- What can you do for us?
- Tell me about yourself.
- What was your most satisfying or your most disappointing work or school experience?

The rehearsal

Practice your responses to these questions. Use a tape recorder and listen to your answers. How do you sound? Weak? Unsure of yourself? Inarticulate? Do you reply in a straightforward manner or do you say a lot of words but never get to the point? Continue to practice until you sound confident and professional. Ask a friend to interview you, using the same questions, but also inserting some unexpected ones.

Video "take one"

Rent a video camera for a day or two and conduct a dress rehearsal. It is an invaluable tool in preparing for an interview. Many graduate business schools, such as Harvard and Wharton, aware of the competitive nature of interviews, have incorporated videotape rehearsals in their interview-training programs.

Act as if this were the real interview. Wear your complete interview outfit, makeup, and accessories. Set up a mock office. Solicit a friend to act as the recruiter. Videotape the entire interview from the moment you walk through the door to the time you leave.

Review the video in detail. Observe your entrance. Do you walk confidently, or shuffle nervously? When you sit down, do you fidget with your clothing; does your hair fall into your face when you move? Do you look directly at the interviewer or do your eyes wander? Is your appearance professional, or schoolgirlish?

Dr. Robert Kent, of the MBA Management Communications Program at the Harvard Business School, recommends this technique for all business schools: "Only by looking at a videotape of ourselves can we really hope to understand how we come across to others. Many of our students are stunned at what they see the first time, and make dramatic improvements in the way they present themselves after a few sessions with the camera."

The interview image

A number of studies by business psychologists show that interviewers (and people in general) make initial judgments about others within the first thirty seconds of meeting them. Obviously, then, you are being judged on superficial factors.

Your appearance and your body language account for more than half of an observer's immediate impression of you. When you speak you are virtually completing the overall impression. What you subsequently say, then, contributes in a minor degree to that initial but lasting impression.

Since so much weight is accorded to the way you look, you must appear as professional and confident as possible. Noble tells Harvard students that "in the '80s, more than ever before, how they look and come across is probably more important than anything else. Let's be realistic—there is a large pool of qualified applicants for virtually every opening."

Consequently, the clothes that you wear and the way you style your hair and even the makeup that you use can improve or diminish your chances of having a successful interview. Like it or not, the world we live in places great importance on image. Or as Harvard Business School's Robert Kent put it, "In many instances if you look the part, you'll get the part."

THE INTERVIEW

Each company has its own interview style and many differ markedly from each other. This disparity can occur in the same industry—and even among people within the same company. Generally, within a few minutes into the interview, you can determine the technique being employed.

There are several distinct types of interviews, and they may vary from a structured direct type on one extreme, to a stream-of-consciousness interview in which the conversation flows languorously from one subject to another.

The basic screening interview

This is a straightforward interview. The recruiter has a prepared list of questions from which he or she rarely deviates. It is mainly an information-gathering situation in which the interviewer reviews your qualifications. The purpose is to determine whether your abilities and style will be compatible with the company. There is very little game playing or manipulating on the part of the interviewer.

You should match the straightforward approach taken by the interviewer. Respond to the questions, but don't be constrained with your responses if you feel that the conversation is not getting around to your strong points. Take the initiative, and emphasize the relevance of your past experiences and accomplishments to your success in the job.

The "Friendly Interview" Type 1

This is a treacherous situation mainly because it throws you off your guard. The interviewer conveys a warm, friendly, low-key approach. While he or she may act sincerely interested in learning about you, in reality, you are up against a master manipulator.

By putting you off your guard, the interviewer is hoping to get to the "real" you. And the approach is quite effective.

While the real you may be exactly what the company is seeking, you may just as easily be lulled into revealing your weaknesses and short-circuiting your job effort.

The consulting firm Bain & Company relies heavily on this approach. According to its former recruiting coordinator Deborah Brayton, "Bain has found that they can get a lot more out of a candidate by putting them at ease. They want to know the real person, not their front."

The "Friendly Interview" Type 2

In another variety of the "friendly" approach, you could find yourself discussing sailing, hobbies, or vacations for the entire interview. You may even conclude that you will get an offer because the interviewer obviously liked you and shared your interests. Chances are, however, that you lost the job within the first ten minutes.

Barbara, a first-year Harvard Business School student, almost spent an entire summer unemployed because of this. She was dismayed that despite a number of on-campus interviews, she had not received a single invitation for a second interview. What confused her most was that she thought she had "excellent interviews," and had established "a great rapport" with the recruiters. Many had even told her how much they enjoyed chatting with her.

Barbara failed to see that a pleasant chat does not make a successful interview. In this situation, the key is to realize that you are being led astray. The interviewer is waiting to see if you take control or allow the limited time to be wasted on "chit-chat." If you permit yourself to be led into a variety of topics unrelated to why the company should hire you, then you are deemed not strong enough to handle the position.

Take charge of the interview. Respond to a few of the irrelevant questions politely and then direct the conversation to your qualifications. This establishes you as strong and forceful enough for a managerial position. Because it tests strength and the ability to take control, this technique is often used on women. Some recruiters still haven't realized that women are as strong as men.

The pressure interview

This one is easy to spot, though never easy to handle. From the moment you begin, the interviewer verbally and psychologically assaults you, trying to put you on the defensive. Occasionally, the "assault" starts unexpectedly in the middle of an otherwise normal interview. You may be grilled with questions implying doubt about your qualifications or abilities to handle the job. Others employ mannerisms that convey a total lack of interest in you; they may yawn or even flip through papers on their desk.

Expect from this tough approach questions like, "What's so good about you?" Or, "Do you really expect me to believe these accomplishments you listed in your resume? Come on now, who really did this work?" This frontal attack, in which even your honesty and integrity may be questioned, usually lasts ten to fifteen minutes, and can be devastating to the unwary.

Other varieties of the pressure interview include the "pop" quiz; puzzles such as the man-hole cover questions at McKinsey & Company; or an interviewer who looks out the window, pretending to ignore the recruit. There have even been instances where the interviewer offers a candidate a cigarette and observes how they handle the fact that there are no ashtrays in the room!** All of these gambits are designed to unnerve and throw you off.

In these situations, you must maintain your equanimity and take control. If the interviewer expresses doubts about your ability, never become angry or defensive. In a calm and confident manner explain why you are more than capable of

---

** The all-time award for a bizarre approach to interviewing must go to a former Dean of Admissions at Harvard Medical School. He would ask a candidate to open the window, which had been nailed shut. In his opinion, by observing the candidate's reaction, he could tell whether they would make good physicians.

handling the job. If the interviewer is working when you enter, take a seat. Wait a few minutes, then suggest that you can either begin the interview or reschedule since the interviewer is apparently busy and you, too, have other obligations.

The curve ball approach

The curve ball approach usually doesn't last for an entire interview. It consists of "zingers," questions that are both unexpected and irrelevant. While they are innocuous, they can be disconcerting. The purpose is usually to determine if you will fit the informal structure of the organization. The following are some of the questions we've encountered:

- What books have you read lately?
- What did you think of them?
- What kinds of music do you like?
- What is your boyfriend or husband like?
- Who is your favorite artist?
- How do you spend your vacations?

As with other types of interviews, the key lies in how you react more than what you say.

Trial by fire interview

This is perhaps the most difficult. The Boston Consulting Group, the pioneer strategic consulting firm, often uses this approach on its MBA applicants. It is more like a PhD orals examination than a business interview.

The candidate enters the room and is confronted by several interviewers. Usually, the person is left standing. There is a blackboard and chalk nearby. The interviewers describe an actual business problem, and ask for a complete analysis and solution on the spot. The applicant uses the board to outline a presentation.

This "trial by fire" approach was originated by the ancient Mayans, who usually ate the losers. While the downside is not nearly as disturbing today (you just don't get the job), starting salaries of $70,000 plus attract long lines of MBAs to the Boston Consulting Group who are willing to give it a try.

The interview wrap-up

Regardless of the types of interviews you encounter, how you handle yourself is more important than the specifics of what you say. The interviewer is already aware of your credentials and major accomplishments. The very fact that you have been called for an interview indicates that you are acceptable. The purpose of the interview, then, is to see how you conduct yourself.

At the end of the interview you will be asked if you have any questions. Do not fall for the old adage that "there is no such thing as a stupid question." This seems once again to be making the rounds of career advice columns and books.

There are plenty of "stupid" questions. In an interview a stupid question is one to which you could have found the answer in the company's annual report. Or a question which hints at your less than total commitment to work, such as how much vacation time the company provides. If you have researched the company, however, and have a specific issue which you would like clarified, then ask—that will impress the interviewer. But keep it brief.

---

*The answer to the question at the beginning of the chapter:

If man-hole covers were square or rectangular, when being opened the cover could inadvertently be turned at an angle and fall through the opening. A circular one can never fall through, no matter how it is turned.

8

SELECTING THE BEST OFFER

Getting on the fast track

S HEILA was young, educated, and arrogant. She was also stunned and bewildered. She had just lost a promotion to another, less educated and less talented, woman.

Three years ago, as a Wharton MBA, Sheila had entered the bank's management training program. From the very beginning, she saw opportunities to upgrade and modernize the bank's antiquated Operations Department in downtown Philadelphia. She pushed and prodded the recalcitrant employees into accepting her business school ideas and methods. And her plans worked very well. At year-end, she could demonstrate impressive bottom line savings. Yet despite this, the bank promoted someone else.

What happened? The young corporate "star" had misunderstood what it takes to get ahead in business. Sure results count. But not to the extent that the novice expects. (And if you doubt this just compare the salary of some CEO's with their company's performance; for example, David Mahoney's years with Norton Simon, Inc. In many instances, it's a case of an inverse relationship—high salary, diminishing profits.)

Business style, or the manner in which results are achieved, counts as well. Sheila's style clashed with the bank's overall conservative culture. Her forceful, almost rude approach antagonized everyone at the bank and overshadowed her achievements. Had Sheila chosen another, more aggressive bank, perhaps one in New York City, she undoubtedly would have gotten her career off to a better start. A little more thought before she accepted the bank's offer, and she might have avoided her current disappointment.

A *buyer's perspective*

People usually spend so much time and effort getting an offer, that once it comes they often think the process is completed. Aside from the monetary considerations, few people pause to consider other aspects of the offer. But, accepting the right one for you is just as important as getting an offer in the first place. "Don't count on adjusting to an ill-fitting position," points out David Maister, associate professor of the Harvard Business School, "because you are a lot less flexible than you think. And if the new job doesn't work out, the divorce will be a lot more painful for you than your employer. So you should be a lot pickier than they."

In the excitement of an attractive offer, don't get carried away and accept it immediately. Even if it is your first choice company, take time to consider it. Use this period to insure that this is the best company and position for you. John Noble, of Harvard's Office of Career Development, recommends taking a second on-site look at the company. "Ask the manager of your prospective division or the personnel department to schedule a return visit. Asking for a second visit is not at all unusual. Many companies expect that candidates for professional positions will want another meeting, and often suggest it themselves."

If you have interviewed at a number of firms, your perceptions of the company may be confused. Your attention and energy was focused on getting the job offer—on them evaluating you—not the other way around. "Don't sell, buy!" says Maister, as now is the time that "you can either buy yourself a job or be bought by one."

"Interview" *the boss*

Arrange to spend at least a half a day at the company. Meeting with your prospective boss should be top priority. Talk with him or her, both formally at the office, and if possible, informally, to observe how he or she acts when relaxed. Lunch away from the office is ideal.

Remember, your interviews are over. You have the offer. Don't hesitate to be somewhat aggressive in your questioning, but don't overdo it. Try to determine your potential boss's work style. How does he spend his typical day? What projects does he have planned for you? What does he think makes for excellence in his department? Remember, this is one of the few times that you will have something of an upper hand with your boss (since you have not yet accepted the offer), so use it to your advantage.

Meet with at least one prospective peer, or better, two. One who works for your prospective boss, and one who does not. Probe to find out what makes the organization "tick" and what kind of reputation your boss has. It will be difficult to get truly frank answers to your questions in these situations (let's face it, no one is really going to open up to an outsider), but you may get some useful information by their reactions to your questions.

Personnel may arrange another meeting with the prospective department or division head. In many instances, the division manager will try to get you to accept their offer that day. (In sales jargon, they will try to "close" you on their offer.) Don't be swayed before you are ready. Complete your information gathering and think things out completely before you accept.

CORPORATE CULTURE FIT

As we have noted, every organization has its own culture. Some are more defined than others. As you move up in the corporation, the match between your style and your company's culture will increase in importance. At some point, no achievement will be rewarded with promotions or raises unless you are also accepted as an "insider."

Once you are seen as "one of us," corporate doors begin to open to you. You will be privy to the inner workings of the organization, you will have credibility, increased visibility, and strong allies. But all of this hinges on the first step—fitting in with the corporate culture.

To maximize your chances for success from the beginning, try to determine the culture of your prospective company. If you are mismatched with your environment, you will find it difficult to manage your job and have little chance of being included in the "insiders" group.

Culture types

Some companies have well-known cultures, and it's easy to determine if your style would fit. Even if your intended company does not have a famous culture, you can still gain some insights into how well you will mesh. Most companies fall into one of several corporate environment categories.

- Bureaucratic cultures: Characterized by clear lines of authority and responsibility. Power is hierarchical, and promotions are regular and predictable. Employees are usually well-trained and operate within highly efficient systems and procedures. This type of company is usually large and dominant in the market and moves cautiously. ITT, General Electric, and the Big Eight accounting firms are examples of bureaucratic cultures. Entrepreneurial, creative, and highly ambitious personalities would not fit in very well with this regulated type of culture.
- Supportive cultures: Usually consist of warm, familial environments. People are open and trusting, they support each other and maintain their relationships with one another both on and off the job. Team players are important in this type of company; "stars" will be out of place. Rohm-Haas, J. C. Penney, People's Express, and Delta Airlines are examples. (During recent hard times in the airline business, Delta employees bought a new Boeing 767 and presented it to the company gift-wrapped with a 20-foot red bow.)
- Oligarchical organizations: Characterized by an exces-

sive concentration of power in the hands of a single individual. Often typified by political tension, nepotism, and uncertainty. Power alliances form around the source of power, and extreme loyalty is expected. W. R. Grace and Revlon under Revson typify such organizations.
- Innovative companies: Usually are typified by a fast, exciting pace. The challenge is constant, and even low-level employees have a great deal of power and latitude to implement ideas. Action and decisiveness count in this type of organization. Entrepreneurial and risk-taking personalities thrive. Many of the high-tech and bio-technology companies fall into this category.

WHEN TO TURN A JOB OFFER DOWN

There are some instances where you should turn down an offer, even if it's the only one you have. If you find yourself in any of the following situations, think carefully before you accept. If you don't, you may be out looking for another job within a year.

The big "rider" job offer

Occasionally you will be offered a position that falls substantially short of what you want. But the company "sweetens" its offer by promising that the position will change in scope "very soon," or that you will be moved quickly to another, more attractive position. Alternately, you may be offered a small salary with the enticement of a quick revision within a few months on the job.

In any of these cases, you are being offered one job, with another attached as a "rider" or amendment to the actual offer. But too often the rider is meaningless and promises are forgotten as soon as you join the company. This type of job deception is usually not practiced by large, well-known companies. It's often smaller, privately run companies which indulge in this type of offering practice in an effort to get good people.

As in all negotiations, assess what is offered at the table—not on what is "right around the corner." You are in your strongest bargaining position before you accept an offer. If you can't get everything you want then, it is unlikely that you will get it later. In business as in life, promises are made to be broken.

If there is no clear job description

Never accept a position that is vaguely defined. When the company cannot delineate the job responsibilities in a precise manner, chances are it has not yet determined exactly what the job entails.

This usually spells trouble. It may be a spur-of-the-moment job that could disappear just as quickly. Or, the position could be almost impossible to handle since no one knows exactly what you are supposed to be doing. Too often the burden falls on the person to "guess" the requirements of the position.

If you aren't allowed to meet with your peers

If the company ignores your request to meet with your prospective peers, and makes only managers available to answer questions, be on your guard. While this doesn't happen often, there are some companies who follow this practice. The reason behind it is simple—they are afraid that younger employees will in their frankness tell you about unpleasant working conditions or low morale. Unless you can determine a good reason for your being denied access to your prospective peers, decline the company's offer, no matter how attractive it may appear.

If the company has a high rate of turnover

Some companies have high turnover because the employees have valuable skills. This is true of training/resume companies whose employees move quickly to capitalize on their credentials. In other instances job-hopping is part of the nature of the industry, as with advertising. But some companies are known as "turnover mills" because employees flee quickly from negative working conditions. Quite often these firms will offer higher salaries than others in the same field. This is sometimes a clue to an unpleasant environment.

During the interviewing process, ask about the percentage of turnover. Find out how long others in your type of position have been there. It's also a good precautionary measure to check with your college placement office, executive recruiters, or with people who have worked previously for the company.

FACTORS TO IGNORE IN CONSIDERING YOUR FIRST JOB

The probability that you will stay from your twenties and thirties through your mid-sixties with the same company in today's business environment is quite low. Consequently, even if the company offers the best pension plan of any with which you have interviewed, don't let that enter into your decision. You will probably never partake of it.

Some companies offer better medical plans, and others even have dental plans. But these should not affect your choice. Obviously it is a bonus if the company you select offers strong health plans, but we are talking about your career—not saving a few dollars getting your teeth capped for free.

Vacation policies should not be a factor in selecting a company, either. It is pleasant to work in a company that offers three weeks paid vacation instead of one or two, but in the long run, your job choice is too important to be predicated on having more time for vacation. Save that as a bargaining chip when you become a hot-shot young executive.

One of the more rigorous interview formats is followed by Procter & Gamble of Cincinnati. While some companies are more aggressive in their approach, and others are far less demanding, the P&G approach is useful in delineating an interviewing process for professional managers.

Each year the company interviews over 23,000 people for entry-level positions. They finally hire less than a thousand. With such odds, any misstep eliminates a candidate from the running. The company has refined the process to such a degree that they eventually recruit candidates who share similar personality profiles and strengths; and yet, surprisingly to its critics, have strong individual personalities.

THE HIRING OF A BRAND ASSISTANT

Consider the hiring process for brand assistants, the entry-level position of the marketing area. (P&G does not hire brand people at any level other than entry. They promote solely from within the organization.)

Most recruits come directly from college and business school. The company sends representatives from various brand groups, in addition to personnel managers, to conduct on-campus interviews. Some of these individuals are from lower levels of the brand management team. But they have been trained in interviewing techniques by upper-level managers who employ films, video equipment, and a variety of interview "games."

Representatives are chosen for two reasons: they are expected to be long-term employees, and they have created a favorable impression on upper management. At the company, it is considered to be a "plum" for a brand person to be selected as a recruiter.

The first cut-off

Astute candidates may realize that the interviewer is at a lower level in the company, but he or she will make a major mistake by treating this on-campus interviewer as anything less than a marketing vice-president. The on-campus interviewer, regardless of rank, has the power to invite candidates to the headquarters for more interviews or to veto them immediately.

The company seeks people who have demonstrated leadership abilities, entrepreneurial drive, and strong career ambitions. P&G places far greater emphasis on extracurricular activities and unusual hobbies or interests than some other organizations. The company's view is that these non-academic pursuits are a strong indication of long-term potential.

The candidate must also take an examination. The forty-five minute test is a combination IQ and achievement test covering mathematics, general business, and grammar. If he or she receives a satisfactory "mark" on the test (the actual score is never revealed) and is approved by the interviewers, an invitation to the headquarters in Cincinnati is extended.*

The headquarters visit

The marketing functions of this $13 billion giant are located at the Cincinnati headquarters. Here the recruit is put through a series of rigorous interviews starting at 8:30 AM sharp. Typically, a candidate meets with two brand managers and a group product manager. As previously agreed, the interviewers each probe for information on a different facet of the candidate. Consequently, there is little overlap in the type of interview questions or format.

* A few years ago, when new employees exchanged stories of their interviews, it was discovered that P&G did not require Harvard graduates to take the test. This led to bitter feelings among some of the employees who were compelled to take the test just because they had not gone to Harvard.

One interviewer may adopt a laissez-faire attitude of "tell me about yourself." This leaves most of the work to the candidate to sort through the myriad of personal information and select specific highlights. A good interviewer can form a strong assessment merely by what the person chooses to relate or ignore.

Another interviewer may be seeking the degree of aggressiveness by setting up a situation in which the candidate should take control. One manager enjoyed using a particular tactic. In the middle of the candidate's discourse, he would walk to the window and stare outside for five, even ten minutes. He was testing to see if the candidate would falter. He was looking for people who would pursue the interview regardless of whether the interviewer appeared to be listening or not. Of course, he was listening closely.

The lunch test

After a morning of interviews the candidate is sent to lunch, accompanied by various low-level brand people. During this time the interviewers are meeting to review the results of their morning sessions. By the time lunch is over, one of three actions is followed: the candidate is extended an offer; cut from the competition; or put through one additional interview. In the last situation, the candidate is considered questionable and a higher-up must enter the decision-making process.

A candidate sent to personnel after lunch is out of the running. (Rejected candidates were not told of this decision. A formal letter of rejection might not go out until a week or so later.) If the candidate is put through one more interview, the decision rides on the results of the final interview. A candidate brought to the office of the group product or advertising manager is given an invitation to join the firm. All job offers that are to be made are done so that same day.

9

CORPORATE FIRST IMPRESSIONS

The pegging effect

THE CONFIDENTIAL FILES are locked away in a special office on the executive floor. Only the chairman and a handful of his executives have access to them. What is this information that Citibank guards as if it were state secrets? It's the bank's management-tracking system. The files contain the names of managerial employees and how they are categorized.

Early in their careers, almost from their first day on the job, young Citibank professionals are categorized by upper management in terms of their potential. Later, they are formally slotted in their files indicating whether they are fast trackers, average talents, or those who never quite got into the race. The category into which an employee is placed means the difference between careful nurturing of one's talent by top executives, or being relegated to the sidelines of the managerial playing field.

At Citibank, the potential stars are labeled Corporate Property; the average employees are dubbed Group Property, and those headed for corporate oblivion are called also-rans.

THE PEGGING EFFECT

Success in any company is rarely the result of consistent hard work applied over a long period of time. In fact, long-term prospects at a company are often determined during the initial phase of a job. Contrary to popular thinking, the first six months in a job are much more than a period of acclimation and adjustment.

During this erroneously labeled getting acquainted period, a new employee is "pegged" subconsciously in the minds of the decision makers in the company. And categorized as a promising, average, or short-term prospect. Once established, this initial image is extremely difficult to change.

We've coined the term "pegging" to describe the process, which is based in great part upon the same stereotypical and superficial principles that come into play when people meet for the first time. (It also plays a pivotal role in the interview situation.) It is simply human nature that people are quick to categorize others, on both conscious and unconscious levels. And very slow to change their minds, despite compelling evidence to the contrary.

It may be superficial as well as unfair, but informal pegging occurs in all companies. (Many firms subsequently take this process one step further by formally categorizing managerial employees, via files, codes, or management-tracking systems.) Ironically, it is the subconscious and non-logical nature of pegging that makes it so easy to manipulate for your purposes.

A period of adjustment?

Many people subscribe to the assumption that the first few months on the job are a time of adjustment, when mistakes don't count and allowances are made for the fact that you are getting acclimated. Few people think that anything you do during this time (short of setting the building on fire) will seriously affect your future in the company.

For the most part, new employees often assume that they are given a tabula rasa ("a clean slate") for the first few months—and that only after this time do they actually become accountable for their actions. Some books and job counselors encourage people to use this time to ask as many questions as possible to "show your interest" in the company. They also emphasize that no one expects too much of you during this period.

This type of thinking is naive, and advice to this effect is dangerously misleading. It is predicated on the erroneous assumption that managers are patient, understanding, compassionate, and logical—in other words, different from the rest of humanity. If you adhere to this philosophy you could find that you have an image problem, and consequently a career problem, before you even settle in on the job.

Day One accountability

We could ascribe logical reasons for the almost immediate effects of pegging. One could be that the company is paying a great deal for you in these days of high starting salaries, and expects performance from the beginning. Or the boss is ambitious and is depending upon you, as one of his new key subordinates, to be an integral part of his plans for advancement. But while these arguments for "hitting the ground running" sound good, they are irrelevant.

In reality, pegging occurs simply because people are quick to form judgments about others. Perhaps this is a throwback to the caveman days, when the ability to determine quickly whether another was friend or foe was advantageous. Or maybe it results from our natural impatience and a need to resolve ambiguities. But whatever the reason, each person tends to characterize immediately everyone he or she meets.

The bottom line, then, is simple. As soon as you enter the building on that first day of work, the scoring begins. And the first six months could be more important than any other time in your career. How you are pegged by the company during this period will set the stage for your future success or failure.

Pervasive phenomenon

Few will admit the existence of pegging. In fact, many people don't even realize that it occurs. Pegging is rarely conscious or malevolent. For the most part it is a subconscious and perfunctory act. And it occurs at every level of an organization and in every type of company or industry.

Consider the new trainee who forgets to handle a detail on one of her projects . . . and the word "sloppy" flashes through her boss's mind. Or she misplaces an important paper and the image of a "disorganized" person becomes imprinted in her boss's memory. If an established subordinate with a positive image did these same things, it would be quickly forgotten. Yet, during this critical formulative period of pegging, these trivial things can set up long-lasting impressions. People often make far-reaching assumptions based on one detail.

The self-fulfilling prophecy

For the new employee, pegging will have an enormous impact on future success. Once pegged, all the employee's subsequent actions are affected either negatively or positively depending upon which category the employee is put in. In other words, if an employee is pegged as a superstar, then the work will be seen in a more positive light. The result is that an individual who is expected to succeed will more than likely succeed. (A simple case of self-fulfilling prophecy.)

More importantly, those considered fast trackers benefit from the special care and attention that the company extends to people in this category. There are exposed to a variety of areas and projects, provided regular contact with higher level management, and encouraged and nurtured along the route to the top. They have a much greater latitude for errors and blunders in all aspects of their interaction with the organization. Not surprisingly, they are promoted quicker and more often.

Conversely, the work of employees pegged negatively will be viewed in a harsher light. Their mistakes are much more apt to "bury" them. These also-rans are promoted infrequently, if at all, and denied the training and experiences offered to the "corporate stars." The actual work from both categories of employees may be equally meritorious if evaluated objectively, but when viewed as the work of a specific employee it will benefit or suffer from the way the employee has been pegged.

Color-coded files

Pegging begins immediately to affect a new employee's prospects. It subtly molds the perceptions of those around him or her. Later, these impressions are formalized, as at Citibank, usually in a management development or tracking program.

Some companies color code their personnel files. One major company uses blue to indicate a top potential manager; yellow for low advancement prospects. In others, pegging is formalized on a boss-by-boss basis. But whatever method the company uses, the fact is that the initial pegging effect exists in all organizations. Only the manner in which it is later formalized varies.

United Technologies Corporation has a special room that contains detailed files outlining company plans for those considered to be potential stars. General Electric has developed a tracking program with upper-echelon executives closely monitoring young managers to ensure that the stars receive appropriate training and grooming for the top spots.

Why all the secrecy at Citibank and United Technologies? Most organizations don't want to discourage those who are not on the fast track. Every company needs its steady and reliable workers as well as its superstars. One lesson many firms are taking from the Japanese approach to management ("Theory Z" et al) is to let every employee think for as long as possible that he or she can make it to the top. This keeps them happy, working harder, and staying with the company longer. At least until the company decides it no longer wants them. And for the "fast trackers," such confidentiality protects them from damaging resentment and resistance from others.

BASICS OF SURVIVING THE PEGGING EFFECT

The critical or formulative period during which pegging occurs varies in duration, but usually doesn't last more than six months. It starts the first day on the job. And ends when most of the people you work with, and for, have become "set" in their initial opinions of you. It usually coincides with the period of time that you are considered the "new person" in the department.

Making the right impression

Anything you do during this period, no matter how trivial, can affect your initial impression. The questions you ask, the way you discuss assignments with your boss, your approach to your first project, and even the manner in which you arrange your desk can have an impact.

If you ask too many questions, if you ask too few, or if you ask the wrong kind you can generate a negative impression. If you forward projects which are late, analytically superficial, or contain a number of small mathematical or typographical errors, you will affect your credibility. (Obviously if your work contains major errors, you will have serious problems.) Something as seemingly innocuous as expecting your secretary to do something that she doesn't ordinarily do could generate problems.

In fact, these first few months are tantamount to walking through a mine-field—the only difference being that if you step on a "job mine," you won't feel the explosion until months later.

Manipulating the system

There is some merit to pegging. People in companies do tend to fall into one of three categories. The problem is that the pegging decisions are made far too quickly and are predicated on very superficial factors. As a result, they are often inaccurate. Success probabilities may be allotted unfairly to an employee because of injudicious pegging. This category placement then colors all subsequent perceptions of that employee's work. This is especially true once these initial perceptions are formalized through management development plans.

For a savvy employee, however, the effect can work to his or her advantage. Since the effect exists, why not learn how to use it to your advantage? Its superficial nature makes it relatively easy for you to manipulate.

THE DESK DILEMMA: CLUTTERED vs. NEAT DESKS   Since pegging is based upon standard external factors, you must project those characteristics that create positive impressions. Attributes that engender a successful managerial demeanor are professionalism, dedication, hard work, initiative (but not so much that you encroach on others' bailiwicks), an ability to interact with people, and a "fit" with the corporate environment.

Yet, these qualities are highly subjective, and like "beauty," are in the "eyes of the beholder." Professionalism connotes different things to different people. One boss's idea of hard work may mean eating lunch at your desk; for another, it's not leaving the office before 10 o'clock at night.

In his recent book, *Managing,* Harold Geneen, the tough former chairman of ITT, declared that a manager with a neat desk wasn't doing a good job. From Geneen's perspective, an effective manager would have a desk cluttered with paperwork from various projects. This would indicate that the manager was on top of things. Contrast this with the philosophy universally held at Procter & Gamble. In that company, a desk with more than a few papers on it is an indication of a manager who does not have the job under control. At P&G, a cluttered desk is a sign of an employee having trouble handling the position.

The difficulty in controlling the pegging system is determining how to project the desired characteristics effectively, since they can be defined differently at each company. If everyone stays late in your division, then skipping lunch to work is not necessarily going to have the desired effect upon your image. If your boss's idea of dedication is starting work an hour early, then coming into the office on weekends to make a good impression is probably a waste of time.

It is important to note here that we are not talking about real dedication, actual hard work, or true professionalism. Whether you really are dedicated, hard working, or professional is irrelevant in many instances to how you are perceived. (Can Geneen really evaluate the effectiveness of a manager simply on the basis of how he or she maintains a desk?) To most people, you are what you appear to be. As long as you can project the impression of these positive characteristics, you will be seen in a positive light.

INTELLIGENCE OPERATIONS The key to surviving and using pegging successfully is knowing what the "right" characteristics are in your company, and simulating them. Observation and perception are important, as well as a good "intelligence-gathering" network.

Start with your boss. What hours does he keep? How does he organize his desk and files? Is his approach to daily business calm and relaxed, or at high-speed? Determine his overall style and copy it.

Look around. How do your peers act? Is the atmosphere in the organization serious, subdued, frenetic, or light? Who commands respect and why? Lunch, after-work drinks, and even casual conversations in the hallway, all provide clues to the right ways to act.

Getting started with the right image

Since we devote several chapters to dealing with your boss, creating visibility, and getting along with colleagues, we will not reiterate detailed strategies here. However, often before you even find out the specifics of your company, it is possible to follow a few ground rules for projecting the "right image" from the start:

· Take your cues from your boss.

You rarely go wrong copying the boss. Observe your

boss's approach to work and follow it. If your boss comes in early, you arrive early. If he works in the office on Saturday morning, you be there as well.
· Prepare for all meetings with the boss as if they were interviews.
No matter how trivial the content of your initial meetings with your boss, prepare for them whenever possible. These first meetings are critical to being pegged positively. Anticipate the topics to be covered. Put together a background file on the projects you will be discussing. Impress the boss with your initiative and desire to become a contributing member of the team.
· Maintain a neat desk and file system.
Harold Geneen to the contrary, keeping your work area neat usually gives the impression of being organized to most bosses. But take your cues from your boss and other higher-ups.
· Meet all of your deadlines on your first set of projects.
It is more important that you meet your first promised deadlines than it is to finish the projects in record time. In an effort to show how good you are, don't box yourself in with unrealistic time commitments. Allow yourself some leeway, but always be on time. If you can, pad your deadline by a day or two and hand your work in early.
· Make sure all of your paperwork looks impeccable.
Any work, whether it is a thirty-page business plan or a two-paragraph project update, should look perfect and be free of "typos." View every piece of paperwork as if it were being presented to the president of the company. Memos are frequently judged more by the way they look than what they say, and your first written work will have an important impact on your boss's subsequent perception of you.
· Be outgoing, project a friendly image.
Be positive, outwardly friendly, and take the initiative and introduce yourself around your department to others.

Don't fall victim to the trap that you can make corporate "friends" later—after you have mastered your job. By then it will be too late. You will have created the negative image of being aloof and condescending, and that you are just another "arrogant MBA." Start right away to establish a rapport by lunching and socializing with co-workers.

Asking questions of the boss

Everyone will encourage you to ask questions in the beginning. They will spout those old favorites, "don't be afraid of asking questions," or "asking questions is the only way you will learn." But some take this advice literally, and in their eagerness to show their interest, ask too many.

Keep in mind that it's difficult for those who have been working for a long time to remember what it was like when they started. Perfectly reasonable questions may very well seem naive. Relying solely upon your boss for information will dilute the amount of effective time you have with him or her.

Obviously, you must ask questions, but start with less powerful sources, such as peers, secretaries, or staff groups. If you want the previous work on your new assignment, instead of asking your boss, ask your secretary. She probably has it all neatly filed. Let your boss marvel at your initiative when you turn in a thoroughly researched project.

If you must ask the boss, keep a list of your questions and review them at one time, perhaps every few days. This will alleviate the impression that you are running to him or her with a question every few minutes. Ask intelligent questions that show some thinking and initiative. This way you won't be perceived as a helpless employee who needs to be handheld at every step.

Special problems for women

Women have even more potential problems than men during the critical image-formulation period. Some male, and even female, bosses still subconsciously perceive women as nice, helpless, disorganized, and illogical.

Since women have made strong progress in the 1980s, we can safely say that the new professional woman on the job is not immediately burdened with this stereotype. However, she is walking a tightrope, and runs the risk of being relegated to it if she gives off even a few wrong signals. A man, for example, can request assistance a number of times before others begin to think of him as helpless; a woman only has to ask a few times before the image of "helpless female" surfaces.

Guard against being seen as "a girl." Avoid making suggestions in a way that sounds like requests for permission. Asking the boss's approval to proceed with a plan also reinforces the parent-child image. Instead tell the boss your anticipated next steps and the reasons for your decision.

Don't bring problems to your boss. Bring solutions. The stereotype implies that women turn to men in times of crisis to rescue them. If you have a normal business problem (not a disaster), don't run first to your boss. Solve it yourself, or seek assistance from a co-worker. Then go to your boss with the solution.

IS A WEAK INITIAL IMAGE THE END OF THE GAME?

As with most problems in life, an ounce of prevention is worth a pound of cure. The effects of pegging are long-lasting and difficult to change, yet easy to manipulate. Make it work for you instead of against you, from the start.

If you have been pegged as a short-termer during the formulative period, is it the end? Not necessarily. But unless you take drastic and determined measures, you will be stuck in that category for the duration of what will surely be a disappointing career at that company.

The first step in reversing a short-term image is to realize that you have created one. Sounds simple, but surprisingly few people are ever aware of their problems until the day they are fired. The strategies for overcoming negative pegging are basically the same as those for creating positive visibility on the job, which we cover in a later chapter.

Knowing when to call the game

Perhaps an even more appropriate question is whether you should even try to overcome a truly negative image. While your initial response may be "yes—don't give up the ship!" and other similar exhortations, we're not so sure.

The world's most successful generals had a knack for choosing the right place and the right time to fight their battles. Most subscribed to the adage that "discretion is the better part of valor." If you have allowed yourself to be pegged as a short-term prospect, you should seriously consider starting fresh somewhere else. Despite valiant efforts, you simply may not be able to reverse your initial pegging, and more to the point, it may not be worth the effort. Your time, energy, and ego may be far better served by seeking a new position.

10

INTELLIGENCE OPERATIONS

How to find out what really goes on!

I T READ like a plot from an Arthur Hailey novel on big
business. The recently named chairman and CEO of a
major corporation was accused by one of his senior executives of wiretapping his office and home telephones. But it
wasn't fiction; the story made national headlines, and the
chairman was Harry Gray of United Technologies Corporation. At stake was the top position of a company with almost $15 billion in sales.

His accuser, the ex-president and former heir apparent
to the chairmanship position, had recently been forced out
of the company. Another ousted aspirant for Gray's position, believed that he, too, had been wiretapped. Both men
claimed that Gray had bugged their offices to obtain information that would discredit them. And ultimately, eliminate
his competitors.

The truth may never be learned. Those executives allied
with Gray doubted the story. Those against him believed it.
But few top-level executives are surprised by the possibility
of such an incident.

KEEP YOUR FRIENDS CLOSE, AND YOUR
ENEMIES CLOSER

We're not suggesting electronic surveillance as a technique to assure progress up the corporate ladder. But to paraphrase the old adage, "in business what you don't know
can hurt you." This is especially true in today's environ-

ment. It may sound like a good idea to "mind your own business" at work and not "meddle" in the affairs of others, but the truth is quite the opposite. Lack of certain types of information can create serious problems on the job. Connecting with the corporate information network, then, is a necessity.

With any newly-acquired position, it makes sense to conduct "intelligence-gathering" operations immediately. This is even more imperative if you are changing companies. Knowing what information to get and how to get it is essential to surviving the pegging period.

When we speak of information, we are not referring to secret or confidential data. Nor are we recommending Harry Gray's alleged James Bond approach to securing it. While such information can be quite useful, your initial objective should involve collecting background information and other nonconfidential data that will give you the "lay of the land."

Locating the power source

It is easy to determine the formal structure of your company. Organizational charts serve this adequately. But such charts rarely reveal where power really exists. In any company, there are several categories of people vis-à-vis power: those who really have it; people who are accumulating it; those who have it by riding on other's "coattails"; and people who never had it and never will.

The right information can help an entry-level manager sort out the real story and determine the informal but critical corporate roles of your company's players. Knowing how each employee fits into the organization's political structure helps determine the people to cultivate, those to treat with special respect, and those to avoid.

Knowing who has real power in the company, whether directly over you or more obliquely, is useful in other ways. You can observe their managerial style and emulate it. You can also seek opportunities to establish visibility with them. Conversely, you can avoid strong associations with those whose negative image in the organization could have a deleterious impact on your own, or who are on the wrong side of a power struggle.

In short, you can maximize your "return on investment" by not spending valuable time cultivating relationships with people who will either have no effect or a negative one on your position.

The lamprey eel, snoops, and other problems

Such a callous approach to business associates may surprise you. But do you want to tarnish an otherwise good start on a job because you were linked with a person considered weak and ineffectual? A new employee is particularly vulnerable. Since you don't have an established image you could very well acquire the negative one of those with whom you associate.

This situation occurs more frequently than is imagined. When a new person arrives in a department, most people will give him or her some distance. The newcomer is considered an unproven "outsider." And, those in power positions will be too busy to give the employee much attention.

But the "duds," those who haven't made it and never will, have lots of spare time. Often left out of things, these people gravitate to newcomers who are too naive to avoid them. Typically, the new employee feels compelled to respond to these overtures of friendship. Frequent in-office chats, lunch, or perhaps after-work drinks follow. Inevitably, the newcomer learns a sorry lesson too late: it is easier to remove a lamprey eel from an unwary aquatic victim than to rid oneself of the attentions of such individuals.

It is also useful to know who is informally connected to those in high-power positions. Many managers or department heads have a "well-oiled" information network, which often includes a "snoop." This is usually someone at a lower level who acts as the big boss's eyes and ears. Knowing who this person is can save one from embarrassing slip-ups.

At Bristol Myers, an older department manager was a long

time acquaintance of a senior vice-president. The manager was well past his prime, and many wondered why the company kept him around. His tenure was secured by the fact that he was the senior v.p.'s information source within the ranks. His snoop role was to provide unfiltered information about lower level employees as well as other middle managers. One of his tasks was to report on his own boss, a group manager. The senior vice-president wanted to keep an eye on the group manager, who had just been installed at the suggestion of the president.

Only after the senior vice-president was assured by his "friend" that the group manager was loyal to him and not to the president, did he accept him. Had the newly designated manager made a thoughtless remark, he may have found himself in a deep freeze. As would anyone else who was unaware of the department manager's true role within the organization.

THE GRAPEVINE . . . AND HOW TO PICK IT

One of the easiest tasks in any company is finding out other people's business. There are rarely any real secrets in an organization. Of course some information may be contained within a select group, but even then, it probably won't be a secret for long since more than one person knows it. If two people know something, sooner or later others will find it out.

To develop a worthwhile intelligence-gathering system, assume that everyone is a potential information source. No one is too low-level. Never underestimate the curious convolutions of the company grapevine. (Some of your best information may come from those below you.) At the outset, establish casual contact with as many people as you can. A few pleasantries while conducting business can reap rewards later.

One enlightening example is the story of the "Manager and the Coffee Woman." Bill, a bank financial services manager, had always been courteous and friendly with Margaret, the woman who made the rounds each morning selling coffee and donuts. Unlike the other professionals, who had their secretaries pick up the snacks, Bill fetched his own and usually exchanged small talk with Margaret. Margaret liked Bill, who did not appear to be a snob. This "relationship" saved Bill from making a serious career mistake.

Bill had decided to accept another company's employment offer because he found his boss increasingly difficult to work with. Just before he accepted, however, Margaret asked him what his position would be following the "reorganization." She had heard the word bandied about earlier by secretaries during her rounds on the executive floor. Bill realized at once what this meant. He postponed his acceptance of the new offer, and was rewarded with a promotion two weeks later when the department was split and his boss was moved to another division.

Never underestimate any potential source of information. Secretaries, receptionists, and those who run clerical and typing pools all can provide valuable information. Even the clerks in the mail room can be privy to inside information.

Saunas: the modern-day water cooler

Any time that people are away from the office or in a relaxed atmosphere is good for information gathering. Use lunch time to develop and solidify contacts. Don't restrict yourself to the same group of people. Lunch regularly with people from different parts of the company. Cultivate associations in your industry. Quite often you'll get information about your company's overall stance in the marketplace. You may hear a different, perhaps more objective, perspective on your firm's activities.

Another opportune time to discover your company's behind-the-scenes activities is when employees get together for afterwork cocktails. When your colleagues invite you for a drink after work, go. Don't stay in the office to catch up on work or head directly home.

If your company has a fitness center, a popular new addition to many corporate headquarters, spend time there.
Employees using company recreation centers have found that
a great deal of information is bandied about while people
are in the sauna or working out. One young female manager
at PepsiCo reports that the new fitness center is a better source
of information on company politics than all the office areas
combined.

HIGH PRIORITY QUESTIONS TO ANSWER DURING YOUR FIRST MONTHS ON THE JOB

Just as it's important to establish information sources and evaluate their reliability, it's useful to have some idea in advance of the kinds of information you are seeking. Below are ten important areas of information that you should pursue when you take a job. Later, when you are established, the list of priority information needs will change.

- Who is the real power in your department/division?
- What are the "success characteristics" in your area?
- What happened to your predecessor?
- Who's in politically? Who's out?
- What kind of power position does your boss have?
- Who are your boss's informal power base connections?
- Who's been fired recently; promoted recently, and why?
- Who has social relationships with those in power?
- Who's having career troubles?
- Which company policies are strictly enforced, and which are ignored?

Social vs. business gossip

Informal information transfer in a company is commonly known as "gossip." It is available to anyone who wants to listen but its accuracy is by no means assured. Nonetheless, it can provide some useful insights.

Many managerial women shy away from company gossip. They mistakenly believe that professionals don't gossip, or that they should be "task/work" directed, rather than politically oriented. Many women also fear that it may contribute to the stereotype of the "female gossip."

There are two types of gossip, social and business. Social gossip usually focuses on the personal, non-work aspects. Business gossip, on the other hand, focuses on work or company activities.

Most sources specialize in the type of gossip they accumulate. Some make it a point to find out about the social and personal lives of employees. While others are far more interested in political intrigue and details of corporate machinations. Both types of gossip have their place.

Knowing, for example, who is sleeping with whom, or who is having marital difficulties is usually the bailiwick of the social gossip. Even this "non-business" type of gossip should not be dismissed or avoided. Such information can prevent you from making negative comments about someone to his mistress. While we are not advocating this tactic, you should be aware that more than one ambitious manager has used the knowledge of a competitor's marital or personal difficulties to sabotage their opponent's career progress.

LOCATING RELIABLE INFORMATION SOURCES

Not all of your contacts will provide valuable information. You will realize quickly who has a finger on the pulse of the company. Some will provide correct information about people and politics virtually all of the time. Others will be more like ostriches, their heads buried deep in the sand and unaware of anything that is going on. Don't discard those who seem to be a dry well, however. Maintain a casual and friendly rapport. Just keep it on an occasional basis. Concentrate on developing stronger alliances with those who are more in the know.

The boss as an information source

While we discuss dealing with the boss in another chapter, it is clear that many people have limited relationships with their bosses. The boss tells them what to do, and they act accordingly. However, given time and effort, you can and should penetrate the boss's shell and set up a more personal relationship. You have succeeded when the boss begins to share inside information with you. This information is usually quite accurate and can be very helpful to your career progress.

Should your boss share such information, it is important to appear nonchalant. Don't ask too many questions, or probe further. Being too inquisitive will make the boss nervous about sharing such information with you (thinking you may pass it on injudiciously). The proper stance is to digest it quietly, and above all, keep it to yourself. Don't trade it with your sources. Nothing will destroy your relationship with your boss faster than being caught betraying a confidence.

In the shadow of power

Another good source about upper-management activities are those not in the power line, but tangential to it. This includes secretaries and administrative assistants, particularly those who work for upper management and those in personnel. These people are often privy to sensitive and useful information. (CEOs don't do their own typing, even on the most confidential documents.)

Many a savvy manager has learned corporate secrets during a few minutes of light banter with the vice-president's secretary. Unfortunately this tactic works better for men than for women. There's still no substitute for the attraction of the sexes. And women will probably occupy most of the secretarial positions for a long time.

Tapping into these sources requires finessé, and it also takes time to build worthwhile relationships. Patience and discretion are key. A pleasant demeanor, a few light remarks when you meet in the corridors or in the cafeteria, and in general a positive pleasant attitude will reap rewards.

When your company sponsors activities, touch base with these people even if only briefly. Your attention outside the office affirms their importance to you and goes a long way toward solidifying a relationship. Professionals often overlook lower-level employees during outside social activities. A secretary who is "played up to" in the office, and then ignored or dismissed out of the office, will not be unaware of the manager's true feelings.

Peers

Peers, especially those not in direct competition, usually share information freely. Since they are on the same level, they don't feel impeded by rank or status. The best contacts are those who have developed strong relationships with their boss or other higher executives.

Having lunch or frequenting the after-work "in" spot with a group of your peers is a good way to tap into this network. It is also useful for getting acclimated in a new company and quickly learning the informal cultural rules and idiosyncrasies. Should certain people prove to be of particular value, cultivate a relationship with them on a more personal basis.

The negative side of peers as a source of information is that they are often as little informed on important issues as you are, and their information is subject to the same accuracy problems of grapevine grist in general.

Time will demonstrate the reliability of your contacts. You will learn to balance inputs from your different sources of information in the organization. Putting these disparate pieces of gossip together will help you to understand your company and its machinations. It will also smooth your way to the top.

11

SUPERVISOR POLITICS

Your boss is not your friend

IN 1965, Walter Wriston, then executive vice-president of Citibank, sent his recruiting executives to hire the "best and the brightest" students from the top business schools. One recruit was 27-year-old John Reed, a graduate of the Sloan School of Management at MIT who had a strong technical, rather than business, background. In less than 20 years, the novice banker succeeded Wriston as chairman of Citibank.

How did Reed do it? Of course, he was bright and worked hard. But Citibank hires hundreds of bright, young, hard working MBAs every year. He had luck—one of those capricious prerequisites for success—and that helped to make him stand out in the corporate crowd. He also took risks, and with his luck, the risks paid off.

But finally, and most importantly, he matched the business style and thinking of Walter Wriston. This bond he shared with Wriston saw him through a few perilous times. It also gave him an edge on the other contenders for the chairman's nod. Eventually, Wriston chose as his heir to the Citibank throne a manager who thought just like the boss.

THE REAL BUSINESS OF BUSINESS

If you were to ask a hundred people in a hundred different positions to define their jobs, you would probably get a hundred different answers. Many would state their job title, others would list their responsibilities, while some would describe the type of business their company pursues. Yet, despite the diversity of their answers, these people all have the same job—to meet the demands and expectations of their respective superiors. In other words, to please their bosses.

As one product manager from General Foods put it: "There are times when my boss has an awful idea. If I can tell him it's bad without getting him angry, I will. But if I can't, then I'll jump right in and work on it. I'd rather 'waste' time on a poor project than make an enemy of my boss. I've learned enough to know that if your boss doesn't like you, you're not going anywhere."

Or consider a financial analyst in a Budgets and Analysis group in a major conglomerate. She may believe that her true job objective is to report the financial performance of the divisions in her billion dollar company. But beneath that rhetoric is her real job. To please her boss.

The boss want her to do good work because he* in turn, is accountable to his boss, and not because he is particularly interested in reviewing financial reports. And so it goes, up the line. Even the CEO of a company must "please" someone, usually the Board of Directors, bankers, or important stockholders or investors.

The successful subordinate

On the job, your world revolves around the boss. The implications of this are quite profound. Nothing else has the impact upon your success as much as your relationship with the boss. Not your work output nor your job responsibilities. This is where most people fail.

This explains why merely doing a good job is no guar-

---

* The pronoun "he" is used in this chapter (and throughout the book) only for purposes of simplification, rather than the more cumbersome "he/she." And, wishes to the contrary, most bosses still are men.

antee of success. Whereas pleasing the boss often is. Many successful people have only adequate business skills, but possess a superior talent for developing a strong rapport with the boss. The "real" business of business is being successful as a "subordinate." This holds true whether you are new on the job, or a senior vice-president with thirty years experience.

In most jobs, pleasing the boss coincides with handling one's responsibilities effectively. But that is not always the case. In some positions, you may find that there is a substantial disparity between what your boss wants, and what one would normally believe the position's responsibilities are.

It all comes back to a point that we have made throughout this book. Success in business is not rational, objective, or fair. Managing people is more important than substantive paperwork on the long journey to success.

Few people view their boss objectively. To some, the boss is a substitute parent, for others an object of respect and fear. In general, many women recent to the business world seem to attribute parental/protector characteristics and expectations to their boss; while men tend to view the boss more as an equal, or sometimes as a competitor.

Regardless of your perceptions, you must learn to deal with your boss. This fundamental requisite of business will never change. No matter how far you advance in the organization, you will always be a "subordinate." And regardless of the actual merit of your work, or your visibility within the organization, success will depend primarily upon your immediate superior's perception of you.

This results from such previously mentioned phenomena as the "chain of command" and "boss centered" cultural factors. As a result of their effects, everything you do on the job is filtered through your immediate boss, who has almost total control of your progress on the job. Since getting along with the boss is so important, we have delineated five strategies for dealing effectively with him.

STRATEGY 1: YOUR BOSS IS NOT YOUR FRIEND

Always remember who your boss is. He is not a buddy, a protector, or a father-figure. He is not a teacher. Rather, he is someone with power and authority over you, who can either help you or hurt you, often on a whim.

Many women enter the business world with incorrect assumptions about the boss, especially male bosses. Throughout their lives women have dealt with men who exerted authority: fathers, college professors, older brothers, boyfriends, and husbands. And, even in these days of "liberation," many women still deal with the male authority figures in their lives in a classically "feminine" manner.

As a result, it is all too easy for a woman to view her male boss (subconsciously, of course) in much the same manner as she does the other men in her life. She expects to be "looked" after and taught; to be given attention, support, and feedback. In return, she works hard to win his approval.

Yet, the boss cannot be compared to a father, older brother, or a husband. He will not treat you as they do. He usually neither likes nor dislikes you, but sees you—and everyone else—only as someone who can be of possible use to him. Your "use" to a boss is usually measured by your ability to produce work which will reflect well on his department. If you can establish a strong performance record at the company, it enhances his reputation as a good "trainer" and supervisor of people.

Unfortunately, some bosses have other, less logical uses for their subordinates. They view them as sources of supplication and respect, or as pawns in their own power games. The work that is produced by subordinates in these instances is quite secondary to the role they play in feeding the boss's "ego."

Because your supervisor is not your friend, you should

not treat him as such. Don't tell your boss your personal problems. Don't ask for advice on personal matters, or cry on his shoulder, literally or figuratively. He's not interested in the particulars of your life. His only interest is whether you are useful for his purposes.

STRATEGY 2: UNDERSTAND YOUR BOSS'S IDEA OF THE "PERFECT SUBORDINATE"

In other words, what kind of employee does your boss want? Make it a top priority to learn your boss's idea of the perfect subordinate, and then become one. This covers a wide area, from your handling of projects, your mannerisms, techniques and style, to the way you act toward your boss.

Determining what your boss thinks and expects is not always easy. People rarely say what they think, and bosses are no exception. Thus, you are usually left on your own to determine what kind of subordinate your boss is looking for. You should consider the boss's attitude in three areas:

- How does the boss view the work portion of your job? What is his attitude toward punctuality or presentation of material? Is he a stickler for detail; does he equate typos with carelessness? Or is he a "big" picture person? Does he expect strong creative ideas, or just rapid processing of mundane paperwork. Does he want to be kept abreast of every development on a project, or is he interested in a subordinate who takes an independent approach? Does he encourage you to ask questions or expect you to find the answers yourself?
- What kind of people does the boss like to have around him? Conservative, blue-blood types? Or aggressive, "street smart" people? Introverts or extroverts? Does he like serious, no-nonsense subordinates, or does he favor a more relaxed view of the job? Does he have an MBA? Is he an Ivy Leaguer? Or does he resent people with such backgrounds?

- How does the boss expect you to treat him? With formal respect and deference? Does he see himself as the captain of your team or as a "buddy"? Does he surround himself with sycophants, or ambitious, self-assured individuals? Is he a strong, confident individual, or easily threatened by others? How does he act with his superiors—deferential or ingratiating? Or does he have a smooth, easy style even with higher-ups? The way he acts with authority figures is probably the way he wants to be treated by his subordinates.

STRATEGY 3: MAKE THE BOSS SEE YOU AS AN INDIVIDUAL, MAKE HIM LIKE YOU

Your boss is not your friend, and never will be in the traditional definition of that word. That does not mean that you don't want him to like you. You most definitely do. In fact, you should work to establish a business "friendship" with the boss in addition to an effective "boss-subordinate" relationship.

In a positive relationship, the boss no longer views you as a commodity that will be of service to him, but rather as a person. Ideally a person that he likes. Unless you have made this transition in the boss's mind, you will find everything more difficult.

During the first weeks on the job, you will be viewed mainly as a commodity. Your strategy to change that should begin immediately. Chat casually and informally with the boss when you get a chance. Lunch time and late in the day are usually prime opportunities for relaxed conversation.

Find out what his likes and dislikes are. Is he a sports fan? A vinophile? A movie buff? People love to talk about themselves and their interests. Explore the boss's personality. If the boss is a skier, then learn enough to be able to discuss skiing. Establish a channel of communication that consists of subjects other than work.

If you follow this approach faithfully, you will find that

the boss will begin to open up to you. To view you more as a person. Naturally, even if you hate skiing, you should learn enough about it to carry on an interesting discussion. And if the boss is a baseball fan, then by all means keep up with all the latest scores.

One successful stockbroker, invited to lunch by her boss, encouraged him to talk about himself. She simply asked him non-threatening questions about his family and his outside interests. Even though the boss routinely lunched twice a month, with a different subordinate, she was the first to ask about his interests. The other stockbrokers never thought to ask the boss about himself. This one tactic made an indelible and positive impression on the boss.

Establishing a rapport with your boss may be somewhat difficult at first. He represents authority and control, and probably, deep down inside, this is intimidating to everyone. Yet, he is a person like everyone else, and can be manipulated with the same techniques that work on your acquaintances or neighbors.

Illusion of friendship

You are actually creating an illusion of friendship. It doesn't matter whether, like some people, you dislike your boss. Regardless of your true feelings, it is the illusion that counts.

If the boss likes you, he cannot help viewing you differently from those whom he sees only as subordinates. He will trust you, and consider you a loyal part of his team. In evaluating your work, or your promotability, he will review you just a bit better. And when things get tough and pink slips begin to fly, you may find this "friendship" saves your job.

While this may appear to be manipulative, it is a necessary approach to any job. And you can be sure that if your boss is smart he treats his boss in the same way. It's good business sense.

Flatter your boss

As Somerset Maugham said, "People ask for criticism but they only want praise." Everyone loves to be complimented. Bosses are no exception. After a brief period on the job you will become aware of the skills and talents for which he is most proud. It may be how he handles his job, his appearance, or his squash game. It could even be something absurdly trivial. Just because a boss is an executive doesn't mean he can't be childish. Consider this example related by a Columbia University graduate working for Salomon Brothers, the New York investment bank.

"I was called into the office of one of the heavyweight partners. He was standing side-by-side with another partner. Seeing the two of them standing there like that, I really thought that I had made a major mistake. And then the senior partner asked me which one of them was taller. Here were these two hot-shot execs making a combined salary of a half a million dollars, and they're squabbling over who's taller. I knew it was a no-win situation. But I figured if I had to pique one of them, it wasn't going to be the top guy. So I said the senior partner was taller, even though he wasn't!"

Corporate mimicry

Another way to get your boss to like you is to imitate him. If he plays racquetball after work—follow suit. If he sees business plans in terms of war (he uses words like "target," "decimate," or phrases such as "blowing the competition out of the water"), make it sound as if you've been in the trenches half your life. How could a boss fail to support an employee who reflects the best parts of himself?

Imitation, it is said, is the sincerest form of flattery. And since most bosses see themselves as managers par excellence, they will have a much more positive opinion of you if you share their traits. In business, opposites rarely attract. Likes do, though. People and bosses are attracted to others who are similar to themselves—it is simply a reaffirmation of their own value.

John Landry, the senior executive vice-president of Philip Morris, was asked why he chose one subordinate in particular to follow his path to upper management. He replied with unusual candor, "He was the closest thing to a clone I could find . . . And I've always had the utmost respect for myself."

STRATEGY 4: DEVELOP A FEEDBACK SYSTEM WITH YOUR BOSS

Feedback has become quite popular with many organizational behaviorists. From their perspective, feedback is a valuable tool for management in increasing job satisfaction and productivity. But we're urging a more pragmatic and active role for the subordinate, in which the subordinate initiates and controls the process. We recommend feedback as a means to develop a solid relationship with your boss.

The first part of the feedback system concerns your career plans. According to Dr. Roderick Hodgins, former Director of Placement at Harvard Business School, "You should always have an outline of your specific career goals established on the basis of five to ten years from your current position. And you should be able to assess how you are performing in relation to these goals at any given time."

Let's take a specific example. If you are a commercial lending officer in a bank, you should know what the standard career path for bank management would be over a ten year period. You should be aware of the average amount of time spent at each level from commercial loan officer to the senior vice-presidency. You should also have a general idea of how each level fits into the overall functioning of the bank.

The second part of constructive feedback is to know what it takes to achieve your goals. In other words what your boss expects you to accomplish in order to move from your current level to the next. Most bosses have fairly strong opinions about which qualities and achievements you need for promotion. But each may have a different perspective. It is up to you to know what yours wants. The easiest way to find out is to ask.

The final step in using constructive feedback is a periodic assessment or evaluation of your progress against criteria required by your boss for promotion. Most companies have some sort of formal review, usually every six months, although some wait as long as a year. But as any ambitious executive will confirm, you can't afford to wait a year for a determination. In fact, you can't afford to wait six months to see how you are progressing. This is where personal initiative comes into play.

When you are using feedback techniques, don't let your emotions negate the experience. You will probably hear some negative comments about your performance. That is to be expected. Even if you have handled your job beyond your boss's expectations, he or she will probably suggest some areas that need improvement.

These discussions should be the most important aspect of your job. They should provide a good understanding of what makes your boss tick and what he expects from you.

The following three-stage approach to using feedback for your advantage emphasizes the need for an aggressive perspective on one's career.

Step 1:

As soon as you have had a chance to get the lay of the land in your new job, tell your boss of your career plans. Emphasize your commitment to your career and the fact that you want to do as well as possible in your job so that you can move on to the next level. Have your boss detail what criteria he feels is necessary to achieve your goal, i.e., promotion to the next level. Set up a broad-ranging plan for development of the criteria and skills deemed important.

Step 2:

Establish a mutual agreement to meet regularly to compare your progress against your plan. At these meetings you should be comparing your self-evaluation notes with your boss's evaluation of your progress. If you have a good grasp of your position, your evaluation should be similar to your boss's. If there are a number of discrepancies between the two, there is a problem. Either you have not really understood what your boss is looking for, or you are failing to implement these criteria into your work. (A third, and a much more difficult problem could be that your boss is at fault. There are bosses who are impossible to deal with on a rational basis.)

Step 3:

Conduct this review at a minimum of every three months. The more often you compare notes, the less chance you have of straying seriously from your path. (This does not mean that you should be asking your boss every week how you are doing; this can look as if you are weak and unable to control your career plans.) At the end of each meeting you should know three things: your career progress to date, your demonstrated strengths and weaknesses, and those new projects which will provide the opportunity to demonstrate your improvement in weak performance areas.

We would add one more suggestion: use the meetings to sell yourself to your boss. It's a great opportunity to point out accomplishments that he may have forgotten or has been too busy to notice. Confirm your esprit de corps with the company and demonstrate your determination to grow.

STRATEGY 5: SOMETIMES YOU HAVE TO JUST GRIN AND BEAR IT

"Leadership is demonstrated when the ability to inflict pain is confirmed." No, it's not the ranting of some third world dictator. It's the corporate philosophy of Robert Malott, chairman of FMC Corporation, the Chicago manufacturer of machinery and chemicals. It should require no explanation as to why Malott was named by *Fortune* magazine as one of the toughest bosses in America.

The magazine quotes one of Malott's staff as saying, "One has to play a semi-Machiavellian game just to function with him. We spend an unconscionable amount of time trying to find out when he will be the least obnoxious."

While Malott doesn't represent the typical boss, he does represent one type that you may very well encounter as you progress through the ranks of management. (It is one of the great disappointments of business life that you can't select and change bosses at your whim.) Throughout your career you will probably encounter small-scale Malotts or bosses with some exasperating idiosyncrasy or another. In fact, a recent study has shown that possibly one of every four bosses in American companies is irrational in his approach to managing.

Since your boss is essential to your career success, you can't merely hope that each boss you encounter will have read *The One Minute Manager*. Thomas Watson, the founder of IBM, was noted for his penchant for instilling fear in his employees. And a number of other well-known chief executives such as Charles Revson, Revlon's founder, were notorious for tough management styles. You may find that any attempts to deal rationally with your boss won't work. Although most advice books seem to have an answer for everything, sometimes there are no winning solutions to a problem.

In this case you have two choices. You can find another

job. Or you can wait it out, keeping your fingers crossed that he will be promoted soon. If you opt for the latter, the best approach is to let the boss throw his tantrums and try hard not to take it personally. While Czars blow up quickly and acerbically, they rarely retain that anger for more than a brief period of time.

FEMALE BOSSES

An increasing number of women have begun to move toward middle management. For the first time ever, there are significant numbers of female bosses in professional positions.

You may think, as a woman, that it can be advantageous to report to another woman. It may be your impression that a female boss will be more empathetic because she has endured the same prejudices and hardships as you. Whereas a male boss could not possibly understand the problems that a business woman has to confront. This simply is not the case.

Women: The negatives

The supposition that a woman boss will be more understanding toward a female subordinate appears to be unfounded. (A 1984 *Wall Street Journal* study showed that most professional women prefer to work for a male rather than a female boss.) And there is a good chance that a savvy male boss will see you as a valuable opportunity to enhance his position in the company. Consequently, he may give you more support and training than a female superior would.

Some people also expect the female boss to exhibit more of the so-called feminine traits of nurturing, patience, and helpfulness. Do not expect that she will display these qualities in any greater degree than her male counterparts. If the woman has been successful in the male business world, there is little chance that she did so without being assimilated into the male culture.

Another problem inherent in working for a female boss is the fact that she may see you as a competitor and a threat, despite the fact that you are on different levels. She may justifiably believe that further up the line there will be only one managerial position "slotted" for a woman. And that you could be vying with her for that same position in a few years.

The Queen Bee Syndrome

Finally, you may encounter a "Queen Bee," a woman who has been the lone female in a particular area of the company and has enjoyed the attention and visibility. While this does not occur at the lower-management levels any more, due to the increase in women at this level, it may be found in middle to upper levels in some organizations.

A woman who has had the corporate spotlight focused on her as the only female can react strongly to the presence of another female. Her benefits from being the only woman are jeopardized. As a result, rather than helping another woman she may secretly try to sabotage her so that she can regain her status. This phenomenon should die a natural death as more and more women enter management ranks.

MEN: THE POSITIVES

Since a professional woman has natural visibility in a male-dominated organization, her boss will benefit from that attention as well. As upper management monitors the woman's performance, they will also be watching her boss. Since visibility is one of the keys to getting ahead, a male boss may want you to succeed since it will make him look good.

Another motivating factor for a man to welcome a woman on his team is that women will often work harder than their male colleagues. Many women feel that they have to prove themselves and justify their inclusion into the male society. To make things even more attractive to a male boss, women will often not try to get all the credit for their work the way men do. What boss could ask for better?

Finally, just as the female boss may see the new woman as a direct competitor, a male boss will probably see another male as a stronger threat than a female.

12

THE CORPORATE CONNECTION I

Dealing with people on the job

IT WAS A STANDOFF and for a while it looked as if it might be a shootout as well. The new president of Butterick Fashions had just been named by the Board of Directors, and the seven senior executives reporting to the president threatened to resign. The new chief certainly had the experience and the talents to manage the company. So, why were these men lining up against the new president? Well, the problem was that the new president was a woman.

Jane Evans faced a problem that more and more women will encounter. Not only were these male executives passed over for a promotion, but they were surpassed by a woman. The resulting hard feelings led to a delicate situation. And could have resulted in Evans being finished before she even started. If she couldn't get the men to support her, she couldn't manage the company for long.

There were a number of ways Evans could have handled the situation. She could have played hardball with the men. She could have even let them resign and then filled the spots with people who were more than willing to report to a woman. But that would have left her without any experienced senior-level executives. Instead, she chose to diffuse the situation with social savvy and humor. The result: not one of the men resigned. And Jane Evans continued her impressive career climb, later accepting a top spot at General Mills.

"NO EMPLOYEE IS AN ISLAND UNTO HERSELF"

Climbing the corporate ladder requires deft-stepping around tender egos, idiosyncrasies, and a variety of often clashing personal styles. The most significant difficulties anyone faces in business are people-related. Rarely is the work itself a problem. Organizational behavior is such an important aspect of management that the curriculum of the Harvard Business School has several required courses in it.

Although your primary business relationship is the one you have with your boss, there are other key players in your company. You need to establish good working relationships with your business associates, particularly your lateral counterparts and support group personnel. As CEO of G.D. Searle & Co. (and former Secretary of the Treasury), Donald Rumsfeld noted, "If you want to do something big, you have to do it with other human beings. I don't know of anything more important than that."

You will never be successful in a company if you are a loner. Regardless of your industry or position, if you are in business you must interact with people. And anyone, from the friendly colleague to the secretary or even the company "dud" can create problems if you don't learn how to manage them.

Most people realize the potential impact of the boss on their careers. But many otherwise astute employees dismiss the potential effect of those on the same level or below. These individuals cannot be ignored on your trek to the top. If you don't learn to manipulate and use people in your organization, you aren't going to make it.

THE SOCIAL CONNECTION

Work relationships are unique. Those at the office should not be handled in the manner that you interact with a classmate, a friend, or people not connected with your work. These relationships require different operating rules. It doesn't matter what your personal feelings are toward your co-workers or company personnel. In the corporate world, you do not have the freedom to associate with those whom you like and to ignore those whom you dislike.

The limits of friendship

Eliminate the notion that people with whom you work are your friends. They are business acquaintances and proverbial fairweather friends at best. They work with you because you are part of the team and by working with you, they help themselves. It may seem as if your co-workers are the exception to this rule and that you have made lasting friendships at the office. But even if people are always dropping by your office for a chat, chances are that once you leave the company, you are nothing more than a memory.

These business relationships have limitations that are not found in good friendships. If you are doing well or if you are in a position to provide career help, people will want to establish a "friendly" relationship with you. If you are having trouble in your job, most will not want to be connected with you for fear that it will somehow tarnish their own professional image. Of course, the ultimate intrinsic limitation to these relationships is the fact that someday you may very well be competing with your "friends" for the same promotion.

This should not discourage you from cultivating them, however. Just accept them for what they really are and you will not be disappointed. Use these people the way that they will use you. Business fosters all sorts of symbiotic relationships, and, you will sink or swim depending upon how well you can adjust to and use them.

Keeping a "friendly" distance

Just as with your boss, interacting with co-workers presents a touchy dilemma. On one hand, you must not treat your co-workers as friends. But on the other hand you must develop a "friendly" relationship. If you keep too great a distance between yourself and your colleagues you will be perceived as aloof or arrogant, and your career will suffer. Colleagues will not include you in their after-work socializing, you will lose touch with the company grapevine, and fail to build a power base.

Try to maintain a personable stance with everyone, even with people whom you think can never affect you. The lowliest enemy in business can come back to haunt you. And often people in the lower positions have time to plot their revenge. (Suppose the mail clerk "lost" some valuable correspondence that you needed sent out immediately?)

You have great control over how your co-workers perceive you. Many of their impressions will be gained from you. Give your colleagues positive information about yourself. Reduce the amount of negative information they receive. The more indiscretions and "slips" you allow, the more negative your image will be.

Assume that everything you tell your colleagues will be passed on. Censor your conversations and your actions. Tell your co-workers about situations that reflect well on you or that speak highly of your abilities. Maintain a friendly relationship with your co-workers but at the same time guard your professional image.

Some guidelines:

THINGS YOU WOULD WANT TO TELL YOUR CO-WORKERS

- Any situation that you handled well. (Extricating yourself gracefully from a horrific blind date is not fodder for management promotion.)
- If you have joined any professional club or organization or you are taking business courses to improve your management skills.
- Any appointment or election to a management position in a professional club.
- Excelling at an extracurricular activity, such as winning the squash tournament at your health club. (Everyone loves winners.)
- Any civic awards or positions you receive.

Keeping quiet

Keep your problems to yourself. Don't cry on your associates' shoulders about your personal problems. Anything that suggests you are not in complete control can have a negative effect on your career. Problems denote weakness and your "secret" problem could reach your boss's ear just as he is recommending you for a promotion.

Don't tell your co-workers stories that connote negative business traits. If you are always bouncing checks and you never seem to balance your checkbook, your boss could be reasonably apprehensive about asking you to handle the advertising budget. Or if the department store failed to bill you for an item and you didn't correct it, your company may have reason to doubt your honesty in business matters.

THINGS YOU DON'T WANT TO TELL YOUR CO-WORKERS

· You (or your husband) are having an extramarital affair.
· Your real opinions about your boss (or another employee).
· You have financial problems.
· Your marriage is shaky.
· You are bored by the city or your job.
· You have difficulty handling your job.
· You cheat on your income tax.
· Your husband is considering a job in another part of the country.
· You are "looking into" other opportunities.

THE SUPPORT GROUP CONNECTION

It is easy to get others to respond to your requests when you have power over their jobs, as with subordinates. In those circumstances, you will quickly get what you ask for. But what if your job entails getting other people to work for you and you have no control over their positions? Such a situation exists between line management and staff positions.

People in line management positions have a tendency to become isolationists. They associate only with those professionals who work in their immediate "sphere," ignoring those in staff positions until they need them. But staff personnel are very aware of the treatment they receive from managers. And they can become troublesome if they feel that you only pay attention to them when you need something.

Cultivate staff groups. For the first few projects in which they have input, go to their offices and talk with them personally. Spend a few minutes introducing yourself and letting them know you on a name-with-a-face basis. Get them to talk about their responsibilities, and subtly confirm how important they are to your work. It is much easier to get someone to work for you if they know you personally than if you are a just a voice on the telephone.

Give the staff groups feedback. Since you can't give them a promotion, give them praise. Although people don't expect praise, they feel appreciated when they get it. All too typically, the special favors that staff groups perform for a manager are quickly forgotten as the manager sits back and takes all the credit for the project. Praise in business is something that should be meted out extravagantly.

When you prepare your memo on a project's completion, include a mention of the staff's contribution to its success. Send a copy of your memo to the staff people with a handwritten note thanking them for their efforts. People will want to work for you in the future when they realize that you let management know how well they're doing their job.

(Everyone likes unsolicited positive visibility, especially with management.)

The wrong approach

The biggest mistake new managers make with staff groups is treating them as subordinates. Young managers in particular have a tendency to be inflated with their own importance and see personnel in staff groups as second-tier team members.

Susan was a Stanford Business School graduate who had achieved academic excellence in her courses. As a woman with strong credentials she was sought by a number of major corporations. She finally chose a prestigious food marketing company on the East Coast.

As an entry level marketing-assistant she devised a highly original sales promotion which she anticipated would garner her a raise and elevation to the next marketing level. Accustomed to success, Susan managed every aspect of her project to the smallest detail. She told the regional sales director, in charge of the area where the promotion was to be tested, how she wanted the plan implemented.

Despite all of Susan's efforts, the promotion failed abysmally. (She got high visibility for the project, but it was all of the negative variety.) Needless to say, she waited a long time for a raise. It was a while before Susan understood why her project, which met all the criteria for success, had failed.

The problem with the project was Susan. She expected that, as at Stanford, she could develop an idea and control its implementation. But she had not considered the "people factor" that plays a major role in every business plan. Susan had treated the regional sales director as if he were a subordinate, someone who had to do things her way. She "wasted" no time on introductory small talk nor did she encourage or heed his input. Susan was a businesswoman in a hurry. As a result, he hamstrung her plan.

Never fall victim to thinking that those whom you offend will put the good of the company ahead of personal feelings. If a corporate antagonist can decimate your plan without being held responsible for its failure, he or she will. More than a few young managers have had their careers derailed by an offended staffer.

THE SECRETARIAL CONNECTION

Your secretary can be a valuable ally or a deadly enemy. She* has a great deal of diffuse power and can have a dramatic affect on your progress and image within the company. Much of what we say of them is quite negative, and may seem tantamount to impugning motherhood or apple pie. That paragon of the trusted, highly efficient secretary who not only meets, but anticipates, her bosses needs exists mainly in upper-management levels.

Let's take a typical office situation. One secretary usually will serve several different professionals. Her secretarial skills are usually not held by those for whom she works. (Nor can a manager, particularly a woman, afford to be seen typing up his or her own reports.) Since professionals must produce plans and paperwork, all typewritten of course, the secretary occupies a key position in the flow of work.

As a result her supposed superiors become dependent upon her. And if they share her with others of equal position, they have no real clout over her. She begins to dictate whose plan she will type first, and whose will sit for days waiting for her to "find the time to get to it." She is courted by the various managers, each of whom wants her to attend to his or her work first. Truly astute secretaries use this situation effectively to their advantage. And voilà, a $15,000 a year secretary becomes the key bottleneck in the work output of $150,000 worth of managerial talent.

For women, a female secretary can represent an especially difficult situation. Many secretaries resent working for

* For purposes of this discussion, we've assumed that all secretaries are women.

women. They see professional women as traitors to their gender, or as outsiders who don't belong in the traditional male role of manager. These non-feminists can also be jealous of the female manager's education, salary, and status within the organization. These same women, however, can be charming, helpful, and efficient with their male bosses.

Secretaries are accustomed to being subservient to men, since for the most part women are still brought up to see the male as a dominant figure. But they are not accustomed to subservience to women, and many rebel at the idea. Female managers must take extra care in dealing with secretaries.

Secretaries also seem to have a natural instinct for evaluating the politics of a company. (In fact, the average secretary is often more adept at this than the manager who spends two years in business school studying organizational behavior.) If your secretary thinks you have clout in the organization, or that you are looked upon favorably by management, then she will be quite amenable to your direction. If, on the other hand, she senses that you are in trouble, you may find her becoming increasingly recalcitrant.

As with others in the organization, don't let your guard down with your secretary. Never let her see you as anything but efficient, confident, and in control. A male manager can display "weakness" and not lose the respect of his secretary. (In fact, he sometimes gains a stronger relationship because she feels "he really needs her.") But a female manager who displays the same characteristics will become an object of scorn. (And confirm to the secretary that women should not be managers.) It's the old double standard in action.

Take the example of a male professional, grandiosely apologetic, who hands in a sloppy memo for typing. Chances are she will smile maternally and act as if he is a helpless little boy. She will immediately produce a flawless document and beam delightedly when he once again says how he couldn't do without her. This tactic, more than likely, would backfire on a woman.

THE HUMOR CONNECTION

Many people underestimate the value of humor in business. Managers today, caught up in a frenetic and competitive pace, often adapt a stern and humorless manner. They seem to equate dourness with professionalism. In their efforts to convince people of their serious career ambitions, they eliminate any vestiges of humor from their corporate demeanor.

But as many who have made the long journey from novice to corporate success will attest, a touch of humor can soften a mistake, disarm an enemy, or even save an unpleasant moment.

Consider the situation that confronted a young William McGowan in the early days of his career. Long before he led the attack on AT&T's long distance monopoly, McGowan developed an ultrasonic device to repel sharks. After a number of discussions extolling the virtues of his product, he finally persuaded some key Navy personnel to view a demonstration. He placed the repellent in the midst of a number of sharks.

But instead of being repelled by the device, the sharks were attracted to it and began to chew on it. Undaunted by this unfortunate turn of events, McGowan announced that he had found an aphrodisiac for sharks. Only a few years later, the ever optimistic McGowan would start a long distance telephone service called MCI.

While many successful men employ humor in various business situations, few women currently feel the confidence and security to display flashes of humor. Women may find it even more useful than men to incorporate humor into their business style. As women move into the upper levels of the corporation they can generate a sense of awkwardness in many male colleagues. Some senior executives simply do not know what to expect from women, and often act like they are dealing with fine crystal in the presence of a female professional.

Managerial humor can be used to defuse these tense or icy situations. A burst of laughter clears the air, and allows attention to be focused on the issues at hand. Humor can also be used to create a rapport with others. A person with a well-developed sense of humor has charm. And it is difficult to feel uncomfortable around a charming person. Once men feel relaxed in her presence, the female executive will be seen as less of an outsider and gain admittance to the group.

13

THE CORPORATE CONNECTION II

Social climbing up the corporate ladder

J EAN AND SUSAN, account executives for a major New York advertising agency, were competing for an important promotion. They had similar backgrounds, but their work styles were distinctly different. Jean was extremely efficient on the job. She used the phone instead of making personal visits, and rarely wasted time on "small talk" when she met with business associates or clients. She was convinced that by working longer hours and producing more, she had a sure-fire success formula.

She was wrong. The agency director selected Susan for the position. Jean, bitter and discouraged, felt that management had ignored her sacrifices and dedication. She later left the agency. What was wrong with Jean's plan?

Jean made a common mistake. She misunderstood the nature of a management position. As a result, she concentrated solely on the paperwork aspect of her job and ignored the "social" side. She was the first person at her desk in the morning, and one of the last to leave at night. While her colleagues were enjoying an after-work drink, she was producing an extra report.

Susan, on the other hand, kept typical office hours and rarely missed an opportunity to engage in business socializing. She was active in organizing an inter-departmental squash team. While Susan always handled her work responsibilities capably, she felt that office socializing and professional camaraderie were also integral parts of the job.

THE SOCIAL SAVVY CONNECTION

At some point in your career, you have probably seen a colleague advance without much apparent effort. From your perspective, he or she seemed to spend as much time socializing on the job as "working." If you are like most people, you were probably puzzled. Like Jean, you may be underestimating the impact of business socializing on a career.

Most management positions require a high degree of interaction with people, as well as handling paperwork. In fact, many successful managers have only moderate technical skills but strong social skills. Rarely, however, is the reverse true. An effective manager may not require technical savvy, but he or she does need social savvy.

By developing the social side of your job, you gain a number of benefits. In addition to making work more enjoyable, you will find it easier to implement plans and increase your visibility to upper management. You will also have an edge on your colleagues when promotion time approaches.

SOCIAL SAVVY ON THE JOB
How do you rate?

There's a lot more to getting ahead than just hard work. "Social Savvy" can count for just as much. Take the following quiz to see if too much work is interfering with your career progress!

1. Your colleagues lunch together twice a week. You:
   a. do so rarely, using the lunch hour to work.
   b. join them except when a real work emergency arises.
2. Your colleagues go out after work occasionally for drinks. You:
   a. use the time to catch up on the day's work.
   b. usually go with them.
3. A business customer suggests lunch after a meeting. You accept and use the lunch to:
   a. review business.
   b. develop a better social relationship.
4. In the company cafeteria, you:
   a. always eat with the same group.
   b. try to eat with people from other areas of the company in addition to your own.
5. Your boss invites you to dinner. You accept and use the opportunity to:
   a. give an update on your work projects.
   b. develop a better personal relationship.
6. Your boss invites you to lunch and you are behind schedule on an important project. You:
   a. decline, explaining your deadline.
   b. accept, even if it means working late into the night.
7. After a meeting, you're eager to get started on your newest project. But your boss starts talking about non-work related topics. You:
   a. tactfully hint that you have a lot of work to wrap up before the end of the day.

b. talk, even if the conversation has nothing to do with work.
8. Your company has an office party. You attend and:
   a. use the party to let upper-level managers know how well you are handling your projects.
   b. mingle, keeping your conversation social.
9. You are asked to join the squash group at work. You:
   a. decline, knowing you have too much work to do.
   b. accept, and use it to develop contacts.

SCORING "A" answers have 0 value; "B" answers have 1 point. If you scored 3 or less, you may be in danger of shortchanging your career. A total of 4–6 points shows good basic instincts, but sometimes you forget the impact of office socializing. And for 7–9, you're a pro at making office social situations work and well on your way to a promotion.

"Let's have lunch"

So how do you sharpen your social skills and demonstrate a managerial style? Let's take the everyday lunch as an example. While the food will never intimidate the chef at La Grenouille, you should lunch in the company cafeteria several times a week. In purely business terms, the time invested can offer great returns.

Lunch offers the opportunity to exchange ideas with coworkers. You may gain a different perspective on your latest project or find a solution to a difficult problem. One of your colleagues may have had a similar problem and can suggest a contact to expedite a solution.

As your colleagues discuss their work, you will develop a broader, more managerial perspective. Group discussions of business problems are the basis for the case study method used by the Harvard Business School to train future top executives. When associates share lunch, they often engage in similar problem solving techniques.

Eating in the company cafeteria also provides the opportunity to chat with people from other divisions. A few minutes' conversation with colleagues from other departments can solidify a working relationship. Nor does lunch have to be confined to the company cafeteria. Many executives from different companies use lunch time to meet in a neutral territory to make deals, discuss business, and even form coalitions. Certain restaurants in New York, such as the Four Seasons, even have special tables set aside at lunch time for specific New York power brokers.

THE ART OF RECIPROCITY

In political terms, business socializing helps build a power base. Being privy to your colleagues' projects and problems, you will have the opportunity to see different areas to offer assistance. In business, one favor deserves another. You can "call in your chits" the next time you need a special favor.

This is sometimes referred to as the "fine art of reciprocity."

Socializing also develops your political sense and creates new sources of information. You'll learn what's really going on, not just what is written in the company's annual report. You'll discover the informal corporate structure, who's on the way up, who is on the way out, and who really has power.

The after-work cocktail

Joining your colleagues for an after-work drink, or socializing, can offer even more benefits than lunch. In fact, when employees are away from the office, they have a tendency to relax and reveal even more about themselves and office goings-on.

Many useful alliances have been formed over drinks. And many important decisions have been made during after-hours socializing. It is no exaggeration to say that companies have been bought or sold, and careers have been made or broken during an after-work drink.

SOCIALIZING WITH THE BOSS

Always accept your boss's social invitations even if it means putting off an important project. You may think that your boss will be more impressed because you choose to work rather than relax over lunch with him. But in most instances this choice will work against you.

Your boss is human, appearances sometimes to the contrary. Declining an invitation, even to catch up on work, may appear to be a personal rebuff. You also risk creating an impression that your job is too much for you. After all, how can you handle more responsibility if you aren't efficient enough to have time for lunch?

As we've seen, a boss's perception of your work is often highly subjective, particularly at the management level. A good personal (yet always professional) relationship will cast your work in a more favorable light. Fair or not, it is simply human nature that if your boss likes you, he will think more of your work. Conversely, a negative personal impression, perhaps created by too little business "socializing," may diminish the impact of your work.

SURVIVING THE OFFICE PARTY

Every year companies have what is euphemistically referred to as an office party. It typically is held during the winter holiday season. And this apparently innocuous get-together is fraught with pitfalls.

For the most part, the office party serves the company's purpose well. It is an inexpensive way of giving the impression that the company "cares" about its employees. It shows that the company has a heart and wants to participate in the holiday spirit.

Many professionals make the mistake of thinking that an office party is a typical party. They expect it is a time when they can relax, have fun, and behave in a manner which they would never adopt during the work day. Nothing could be further from the truth.

The company party is one of the few times when people from all levels mingle. It may be the only time that a member of upper management actually sees you in person. The way you handle the party could be the only image that sticks in the president's mind when the time arrives to sign-off on your promotion. The party, then, is not the time to have a high profile.

The office party is also fodder for weeks of company gossip. Nothing is missed under the watchful eyes of your colleagues. Even a minor indiscretion—one drink too many, excessive physical familiarity with a male colleague—and you can be the subject of gleeful conversation.

Partying with panache

- Always attend. Some professionals, aware of its superficiality, opt to avoid it. This is a mistake. The company expects you there as a show of loyalty and team spirit. To forego it could antagonize management and even your colleagues, who may assume you are snubbing them.

· Limit yourself to one or two drinks. Or, preferably, sip a club soda with a lime, which gives the appearance of a cocktail. People who are drinking feel uncomfortable around others who aren't. It makes them feel guilty and they will end up resenting you for it. Conversely, if you have too much to drink, you will ruin a professional image.

· Don't do or say anything that you wouldn't want anyone at the party to notice. Be aware that every move you make and everything you say may be watched and evaluated.

· Leave alone, or with another woman. If you leave with one of your male colleagues, even if you both go directly to your respective homes, people will assume the worst. (The worst is always much more entertaining.)

· Stay at the party only long enough to engage in small conversations with various colleagues and make your presence known. Then leave. By the time someone starts to dance with a lampshade on their head, you should be long gone.

14

CORPORATE FAUX PAS

Slipping and sliding on the fast track

IN THE CLICHÉ-RIDDEN STORY of William Agee and Mary Cunningham, Agee, who had played politics hard and fast for years, made a number of mistakes. But the question of "Did they or didn't they?" aside, Agee's poor handling of the situation in the beginning set off a series of missteps that eventually culminated in the Bendix-Martin Marietta debacle. And Agee's unceremonious termination.

Having been dubbed a golden boy, Agee's spectacular rise to the top of a major corporation was well-chronicled. As one of the youngest CEOs in the country, he seemed destined to join the ranks of business legends. Then it all started to fall apart. Rumors began to spread throughout Bendix that he and his female vice-president were having an affair. And the once sure-footed Agee made a strategic, ultimately fatal, misstep.

At a Bendix business meeting, Agee brought the behind-the-scene rumors to the forefront of everyone's attention. He denied that he was having an affair with Cunningham. And human nature being what it is, everyone was then convinced that they were indeed involved. Those Bendix employees who hadn't heard the rumors were definitely aware of them after the meeting. To make matters worse, once the rumors were publicly addressed at the meeting, the story was quickly picked up by newspapers across the country.

Agee should have known better. The best approach to such a situation is to ignore the gossip while at the same time taking measures to ensure that no future actions give credence to the rumor. The more one denies such a story, the more people are reminded of the Shakespearean line "The lady doth protest too much."

Serious and not so serious mistakes

There are many mistakes that one can make on the job, but some are more important than others. We're not focusing on errors in paperwork. Rather we are talking about tactical and strategical mistakes. While too many technical errors will hurt a career, tactical and strategic missteps usually have much greater impact.

As is always the case, an action which is an error at one company may constitute acceptable behavior at another. Errors are such only in the context of the specific environment. Generally there are two types of tactical/strategical errors: the trivial, demerit type error, and the more serious, job-threatening mistake.

Calling in sick on the "wrong" days, taking too long a lunch hour, or leaving early when everyone else stays late are examples of small mistakes. Not conforming to company idiosyncrasies, like keeping a clean desk, are other minor ones. But even these trivial slip-ups can become serious if they are continued.

The more serious, possibly fatal, errors usually involve the injudicial handling of a political situation. These missteps often create a negative impression that is difficult, sometimes impossible, to erase. At each performance review the error is resurrected in the minds of those who make promotion decisions.

These errors can include by-passing the chain of command, being caught in a serious lie, alienating an important higher-up, being caught shopping around for another position when the boss has been grooming you for a promotion, or threatening to leave the company as a bargaining chip for a salary increase.

TRIVIAL ERRORS

At first thought, most people would not consider errors of this type worth mentioning. These slips may not sound serious, and as isolated incidents they are not. But there is a limit to the number of these minor errors one can make before a general impression of ineffectiveness is created and a position is jeopardized.

Corporate quirks

As discussed in the chapter on corporate culture, every company has unwritten rules which employees are expected to learn (often by osmosis) and follow. Some of the behavioral standards are merely quirks in the corporate personality. These quirks, or idiosyncrasies, are a key component of your company's culture. "Idiosyncrasies" is an appropriate term because these rules form a behavior pattern that usually has no basis in logic or on the realities of the business. They are simply cultural behavior norms that over time have come to be accepted.

Although from a pragmatic perspective these "rules" are usually irrelevant, they are important to your acceptance and success in an organization. For example, some excellent people have been passed over for promotions because they consistently took lunch hours that exceeded the company norm. This trivial error gave rise to an erroneous assumption—that they were not as serious as their colleagues and that they held themselves apart from others. Consequently, they didn't deserve a promotion. From the company's perspective, acquiescence to idiosyncrasies indicates a desire to "fit," or perhaps more to the point, not playing along demonstrates the "wrong" attitude on your part.

Loss of individuality

This subtle pressure to make employees conform is considered by some to be the elimination of individuality and personal expression within the corporation. To a great extent the "individual" must be eliminated for a company to operate smoothly. Few organizations can run successfully when each employee feels free to express his or her individuality. Companies simply are not designed to foster or preserve individual identity.

In one sense, the contemporary corporation can be likened to the society which the author Ayn Rand railed against—where the "we" is more important than the "I." Forget the philosophical ramifications—if you have elected to work for a company, you have chosen to work as part of a group, a cog in the great "wheel" of the organization. Submerging your own identity is simply part of the deal.

Since these idiosyncrasies can vary dramatically between companies, it is impossible to list them. The important point is to realize that your organization will have them. As soon as you begin working for a company, observe your co-workers. You should be able to determine patterns of actions which most people seem to follow. In other words, look for the common denominators in their behavior. If most people adhere to an action, chances are it is expected.

The care and feeding of the company desk

Consider the central item in a typical employee's world—the company desk. At Procter & Gamble's headquarters in Cincinnati, employees must place all paperwork in their desk and lock every drawer at the end of the day. Periodic checks are conducted by the advertising manager personally during late evening hours to see if anyone failed to perform this task. One inconsequential paper left on the desk is grounds for reprimand. Although the corporate offices are securely guarded, and no one is admitted without security clearance, the company philosophy enforces strict secrecy.

Contrast this with certain divisions at W.R. Grace's New York office. In this company, locking your desk is frowned upon by management. The corporate culture here focuses on the problems engendered when an employee is out of the office. "What if you were sick and someone had to follow up on your projects?" is the operating logic here. Although clearly someone will have a duplicate key, the correct behavior is not to lock the desk.

The state of your desk during the day is another interesting idiosyncrasy. In some companies, a neat desk is one step below "godliness." In others, a sloppy desk is a sign of genius. The point here is that by not conforming you are making a trivial type error. It won't get you fired, but it will accentuate your differences with the norms of the organization.

The invisible stop watch

Another area for potential mistakes is the organization's schedule. In most management positions, you are expected to be at the office earlier and to stay later than the official hours.

If your boss and colleagues are in the office by 8 AM, you should arrive then as well. Rationalizing that you can arrive later because you work later than everyone else won't get you far. Nor will the fact that the official starting time is 8:30 AM. It's not the amount of work here that is important, it is conformity. You won't be fired if you come in at the "official" starting time every morning, but your non-conformity will work against your success.

Work schedules can also include weekend attendance. In one marketing company, in which the managers prided themselves on their dedication to hard work, it was an unwritten rule that brand people showed up in the office on Saturday mornings. For those who failed to appear, subtle peer pressure was provided on the following Monday in the form of "good natured" chiding. But the message was clear . . . "you're not one of us."

In only a few instances was working on the Saturday morning necessary or desirable. In fact, many employees spent the time making personal long distance calls at the company's expense, or rehashing the events of the previous evening's party. The key point in the Saturday morning effort was that it was simply an exercise in conformity and team spirit.

Give until it hurts

Some of the above-mentioned idiosyncrasies are found at many companies. Other behavioral patterns are more difficult to spot. At one major Midwest firm, donations to the United Way take on a significance well beyond the actual act of donation.

Once a year, employees are given cards to specify their contribution to the United Way. No written recommendations are made by management and many new employees feel free to decide whether they wish to participate and to what extent.

In fact, they have no choice. All employees are expected to contribute one percent of their salaries. Those who do not check "1 percent" on their "voluntary" contribution cards are invited to the advertising manager's office for a "friendly chat." He urges that they comply with the company's efforts to achieve "100 percent full participation" for the "well-being of the community."

Of course, these employees could still refuse. But, the message is clear. Not helping the company maintain its "unanimous corporate contributor" distinction indicates a poor attitude and lack of company spirit. And results in a tarnished image with management at promotion and raise time.

Rectifying the small mistakes

Minor transgressions can be easily handled. Most can be summarily rectified by ceasing the incorrect behavior, and by avoiding new mistakes.

The key to overcoming small mistakes is to realize that you have violated the norms of the company. Once you know that you have erred, act quickly and positively. For example, showing up late for meetings once or twice can be offset by making a concerted and obvious attempt to arrive early for all future meetings.

MAJOR ERRORS/CAREER SUICIDE

Career suicide may seem like a melodramatic term for committing a serious mistake. But, unfortunately, it is often appropriate. Serious mistakes vary from company to company, but they usually have similar effects. They strike deep at personal credibility on the job, and have long-lasting impact on image and future prospects within the company. Such was the case of William Agee's vocalizing his non-affair—his managerial wisdom and common sense were called into question.

While the repercussions may not be immediately fatal, more than a few in close succession are usually terminal. (Note that we define a serious mistake by the fact that it has a long-term impact upon your image at your company, not whether it is serious from an objective standpoint.)

Again, the situation depends upon the company. At one firm, located in Kansas City, it was discovered that a married middle manager was having an affair with one of his junior-level managers. This was a major scandal to a company that prided itself on middle-class values. The woman was forced to resign.

At another company, in New York City, an identical interoffice romance was terminated by management with no long-lasting repercussions for the participants. The problem in the New York case, from management's perspective, lay in the fact that a manager was involved with one of his own subordinates. The moral aspect of the affair was irrelevant.

The company's "hot buttons"

Potentially fatal errors often strike at the most fundamental ideologies or philosophies of a company. In other words, hitting the company's sensitive spots or "hot buttons." In a company that is fanatically concerned with security, for instance, a violation of this type could have serious ramifications. An employee working on a new project could jeopardize her career by discussing details with someone outside the company, or even with an employee in another division.

Other organizations are fanatical about salary information. Simply disclosing your salary to fellow employees is grounds for dismissal. In a company that espouses "high moral standards," anything that deviates from the middle-class norms impairs one's credibility.

The boss revisited

Quite a few serious mistakes involve your relationship with the boss, and we've discussed many of them in another chapter. Since you spend so much time with your boss, it is easy to become too relaxed and slip-up. One very common error is betraying a confidence. Usually, with time, most people build a rapport with the boss that inspires being entrusted with confidential information. When you reach this point, you may find yourself privy to interesting information. But if you make the mistake of passing it on to others, it could permanently impair your relationship with your boss.

Others don't realize the degree of loyalty that most bosses expect from their subordinates. Being caught in any action that appears disloyal could derail your relationship. Complaining to others about your boss, lobbying with higher-ups for a transfer, or even exploring a job offer from another company can be seen as betrayal.

By-passing the chain of command, either intentionally or inadvertently, can alienate the boss. Many people slip and talk informally to a higher-up about subjects that should only be discussed with their immediate supervisor. Voicing even a small complaint about work being assigned by a boss, or discussing tentative projects the boss has not yet cleared with management, are a few such blunders.

Business blunders and disasters

Everyone makes mistakes on the work aspects of the job. It is impossible to avoid them. Your reports will have "typos," you will forget an important deadline, or botch a key negotiating session with an important client. Surprisingly, even serious work-related blunders can be survived with little or no long-term career damage. It all depends upon how they are handled.

THE $100,000 BLUNDER   Your immediate actions when disaster strikes will have an important impact on your survivability. While many people try to pass the blame onto others (the "cover-your-posterior" mode), this is not always the best strategy. A study conducted by the North Carolina-based Center for Creative Leadership compared the careers of 20 successful executives with those of 20 "derailed" executives from the same companies. All had made mistakes. But those whose careers were impaired had tried to blame others, or had tried to hide their mistakes. Those who continued on successfully had confronted their errors, and acted to reduce the damage.

Roland was a marketing assistant for a Los Angeles-based food marketing company. His project was to develop a promotion to boost sales in an important district where market share was declining. His promotion involved a coupon offer which allowed the consumer to receive a set of dinnerware. Only after $100,000 worth of dated in-store material was developed, did Roland find that another brand group was preparing an identical promotion in the same district. Since Roland had failed to file a required report, company policy dictated that only one promotion could be run, and the other division had priority.

Roland knew that he had erred before his boss or anyone else in his division. He realized that the information would become common knowledge soon, and that procrastinating would just make things worse. He took the courageous step, accepted all the blame, and went into high gear to minimize the loss. Due to his judicious handling of the matter, he was promoted on schedule.

DAMAGE CONTROL   In comparison to the mistakes of the executives studied by the Center, Roland's oversight was small. But his actions following his discovery of the problem demonstrated the same positive qualities that the study's successful managers exhibited. All confronted their mistakes, acted quickly to diminish their impact, and notified their colleagues of the impending problem. The end result is that their actions helped to keep matters under control.

The business world is full of stories in which managers made enormous and expensive mistakes, and still went on to top positions. Another study done by the Center focused on 86 "Fortune 500" senior level executives. It found that fully two-thirds had missed promotions, had been exiled to other divisions, had engaged in a major conflict with their bosses or, in general, had been overwhelmed by their jobs at some point in their careers. Yet they overcame these difficulties and went on to success.

SHOULD YOU EVER LIE?   Many situations are not as clear-cut as Roland's case. He was to blame, everyone knew it, and no amount of fancy footwork was going to change that. On the other hand, it is frequently possible to side-step responsibility for a problem. Or stick another department with the blame.

Generally speaking, consider deception when it is a relatively inconsequential mistake and not worth your boss's or management's time to pursue it further. Without trying to proselytize, you should be aware that people in business lie every day. In fact, if Diogenes were searching for his honest man in corporate America, he would run out of candles before he found one.

Some might choose to see this in a moral light. But if a lie, or passing the "buck," can extricate you from a messy situation and keep your credibility intact, then you must determine which is more important to you. Your morals or your position. If you value your job more, lie. As Bertolt Brecht said, "First comes fodder, then comes morality." If, however, you place greater value on your integrity, don't. It's an unfortunate dilemma but one that must be faced often in business.

When the mistake is serious and management most likely will investigate further, don't lie. You have a good chance of retaining your professional image if you act swiftly to preclude as much fallout as possible. But with a lie, you ultimately will be caught, and the resulting loss of credibility will kill your career at that company even if the mistake doesn't.

HOW TO LIE   Being a convincing liar is a valuable trait in business. You will be called upon to use it regularly. Whether in telling the boss that his baby's pictures are really "adorable" (when in reality the baby is a diminutive Quasimodo), that you are sick (when you want to go skiing), or that the project you have been working on for weeks is on schedule (even when you really don't know how you're going to pull it off on time).

The first step in successful deception is to remember that obfuscation is better than an outright lie. When confronted with the need to lie in order to cover yourself, it is much better to give an ambiguous or oblique answer than an outright, unequivocal lie. Always leave yourself maneuvering room or the possibility for "misunderstanding."

Unless you have tried this approach, you will not realize how easy it is to deceive without resorting to actual outright untruths. People frequently hear what they want to hear, and bosses are no exception.

When you must lie outright, remember the simpler the lie, the better. Don't bog yourself down with a complicated falsehood. Not only is it harder to pass off, but it is easy to forget and trip yourself up later. Stick to the truth as much as possible, and stretch the truth only at the key points.

Is there life after a major mistake?

The problem with major faux pas, as opposed to the other class of errors we explored, is that they strike at one's image. Your image has a profound impact on how you are perceived in everything you do. And once your image is tarnished, it is very difficult to correct.

How do you overcome a series of major mistakes? Perhaps a more relevant question is whether you should even try. Major mistakes take a long time to dim in the memories of those who count. Even people who have trouble remembering your first name will remember your "Big Mistake." It will hound you with the tenacity of the mythical Harpies. As a result, your time and efforts would probably be better applied toward enhancing a good image at a new company, rather than erasing a negative image at your current one.

Steve, a junior-level financial analyst, spent five years trying to atone for a "fatal" mistake. He joined a major New York-based pharmaceutical firm at the same time as Mike. They became friends, both on and off the job. Then Mike began to move quickly in the organization, due mainly to his uncanny political sense. Within a year, Mike was the departmental manager; within three years, a divisional controller.

Steve was slow to grasp the significance of these changes. To others, Mike was now the "big boss." But Steve had been friends with Mike for too long, and was all too aware of Mike's limitations. He couldn't switch into a subordinate-boss relationship with Mike.

Annoyed with his former friend's apparent lack of respect, Mike moved to have Steve "squeezed" out. In this company, though, it was difficult for a boss to fire someone without concrete examples of poor performance. Mike gave hints, snubbed Steve, gave him weak reviews, and nagged him wherever he could. In short, he did everything he could to get Steve to leave of his own accord. But Steve stubbornly refused to get the message.

Finally, after three years "in the cold," Steve's fortunes began to change. The company was computerizing its financial reporting system, and Steve was a superb programmer. He skillfully updated and computerized the entire company's financial reporting system. When the president of the company congratulated Steve on his achievements, Mike, ever the politician, brought Steve back into the fold. Steve was financially back on track, and received a promotion and large salary increase in short order.

Steve overcame a fatal mistake, antagonizing a "big boss." But at what cost? He spent a number of years in the same position at the same salary. He endured the psychological trauma of being an "outsider." He received no positive reinforcement, and had to watch as his peers surpassed him.

He would have been better off realizing that his time was more valuable than to waste it trying to rectify a critical error. Had Steve moved to another company and worked as hard, he undoubtedly would have been promoted several times and received more raises during the same period.

Part Three

ADVANCED STRATEGIES:

CORPORATE

BRINKSMANSHIP

15

CREATING VISIBILITY

The paths to glory

If a man . . . make a better mouse-trap than his neighbor, tho' he build his house in the woods, the world will make a beaten path to his door.　　　　　　　　　　　　—RALPH WALDO EMERSON

THIS ADAGE was coined in the days when there was only one "mousetrap" and long before Madison Avenue. Today, it's more important to have a superior advertising and publicity campaign than to market a superior product.

Even the casual observer of contemporary society cannot help noticing that the world runs on hyperbole and self-promotion. One example of this phenomenon is found in Hollywood. Stars are made overnight with the talents of super-managers such as Jay Bernstein, who has made millions making others famous.

Bernstein's genius is that he can take unknown and often minor talents and make them household names through clever manipulation of publicity. Had these celebrities, like a pre-"Three's Company" Suzanne Somers, relied on their actual talents to get to the top, the chances that they would be successful are slim. At the very least, it would have taken them far longer to work their way to stardom than it did with a well-managed publicity campaign.

The business world is not all that different from Hollywood in many respects. Sure there's less dazzle (although you can't prove it by the lives of flamboyant executives such as Donald Trump, the real estate entrepreneur or David Mahoney, former chairman of Norton Simon, Inc.). But the mechanism for becoming a "star," whether in the board-room or on celluloid, has amazing similarities. Instead of publicity, the would-be corporate star is looking for visibility.

"VISIBILITY" DEFINED

Business does not adhere to the right-of-ascendancy as a monarchy does, except in some privately-owned companies. But merit and hard work don't result in automatic promotions, either.

Consider the results of a recent study showing that the most successful executives spend about 50 percent of their time in the office actually working (processing "paperwork"); and the other half of their time promoting themselves and their achievements within the organization (creating "visibility"). They realize that doing a good job means little if no one knows about it. It seems that while the "meek shall inherit heaven," they don't get the top positions.

Visibility in the corporation can be defined as having top management, or key "decision makers" *other* than your boss, aware of you. It should be obvious that there are two types of visibility, positive and negative. Positive visibility is the type which enhances your image in the eyes of management (and throughout the company in general) as someone with executive potential. Negative visibility is getting noticed for actions that neutralize your long-term potential. As we have discussed previously, your image has a profound impact on how everything you do is subsequently perceived.

A corporate "star"

In this chapter, we will focus on practical tips for the art of creating visibility—demonstrating to management above your boss, and to the company in general, that you are an up-and-coming employee with real potential. In short, that you are a corporate star ready to be discovered. This objective is best implemented with a well-planned and executed campaign. Those who only sit and wait for the corporate spotlight to find them are lost.

STRATEGY 1: LOOK THE PART

Creating visibility is difficult since contact with upper management is sporadic and unpredictable. Frequently the image you create is based simply upon your external appearance and a few brief moments of conversation. For that reason, how you look is a good place to start any discussion of visibility.

While appearance has always mattered, in these days of sophisticated dress and corporate competitiveness, it is now of paramount significance. As one personnel director for a commercial bank put it, "Let's face it, MBAs are a dime a dozen today, even from the top schools. We can afford to be choosy. So we want the total package—credentials, personality, style, and looks." Many companies even rate their employees on their appearance. For consulting firms, like the Boston Consulting Group and McKinsey & Company, one's "presentability" is just as important as one's business acumen.

Sally, a Columbia Business School graduate, landed a prestigious position with a major strategic-consulting firm in Boston. Although she had strong analytic ability, Sally's appearance lacked the style and sophistication that were central to her firm's image. Despite a number of hints from the personnel department, she continued to discount the importance of her image. She was convinced that her work and achievements were the only things that counted.

But Sally's appearance contrasted negatively with that of her consulting team. The managing partners became increasingly reluctant to include her in their outside meetings. She just wasn't, to use their term, "client presentable." Her role was gradually decreased until Sally was considered dispensable.

STRATEGY 2: MAKE YOUR BOSS YOUR PUBLICITY MANAGER

Creating visibility within the company is not something that should conflict with your plans to build a sound and useful relationship with the boss. In fact, your boss should be playing a key role in these efforts.

If your efforts are successful, your boss will provide opportunities for exposure to his boss and to others in positions of authority. He or she should include you in meetings on the executive floor, and comment favorably on your performance to others. In other words, your boss should be your "booster" with those who count in the organization. He should do more than simply use you as a resource in his own efforts to get ahead.

Achievement of these objectives is the most difficult and demanding aspect of dealing with your immediate supervisor. Endeavor to make your boss champion your "cause" with his superiors. Strong reviews and salary increases don't guarantee that he will recommend you for an important promotion. Nor does it follow that simply because he likes you that he will suggest you as his replacement when he is promoted.

If you have followed the strategies in this book, you should have developed a strong foundation for your relationship with your boss. But don't wait for him to provide the extra push you want. Give a subtle prodding. After some time on the job, suggest accompanying him to meetings with the higher-ups, especially if your projects are being discussed. Make sure that you are well-prepared.

Play on the boss's ego. Try to promote the concept of the boss as a trainer, as a role model. Inculcate the idea that if you are successful, it will reflect favorably upon his talents as a manager. Push gently but consistently. He is probably willing to champion you with others, but needs to be encouraged and reminded.

STRATEGY 3: WHEEDLE YOUR WAY INTO HIGH-VISIBILITY PROJECTS

Most management jobs have some flexibility. Expand the scope of yours. Keep tabs on company and industry trends. Look for projects which are connected with these areas of increasing importance. If some important projects are "brewing," try to get involved. Drop suggestions to your boss or to others in the department. Especially if you have some special expertise that would come in handy.

Suggest projects. They don't have to be "blockbusters." In fact, it is better if they are achievable in a fairly short time frame. Ideal projects are quick and easy to complete, and yet will attract favorable attention upon completion. (In other words, projects with high "PR" value.)

Many corporate superstars have attained top positions mainly on the basis of their connection with successful projects. At Ford, Lee Iacocca was associated with the phenomenally successful Mustang. John Smale, chairman of Procter & Gamble, received company-wide attention when, as the Crest toothpaste brand manager in the 1950s, he secured the endorsement of the American Council on Dental Therapeutics. (The famous and oft-repeated, "Crest, when used in a program of conscientiously-applied dental hygiene, has been shown to be an effective decay-preventing dentifrice.") This marketing coup made Crest the number one toothpaste.

In some instances the executives were only peripherally involved with projects which helped catapult them to the top. Consider the adept maneuvering of John Sculley, former president of PepsiCo and now president of Apple Computer. Throughout the industry, Sculley is identified with the very successful "Pepsi Generation" advertising and promotion strategies. In reality, these were already in use before Sculley got involved.

As a result of her connection with several major films,

such as the *China Syndrome*, Sherry Lansing became the first woman to head a major studio, Twentieth Century-Fox. But some of the key projects that she is known for were actually the result of the efforts of her predecessors.

STRATEGY 4: TOOT YOUR OWN HORN

It is simply a fact of business life that you cannot rely on anyone else to extoll your virtues. Magnanimity of spirit is not a common commodity in the business world. If you want others to know of your achievements, you must tell them. In other words, "toot your own horn." You will be in good company. Most of the successful people throughout the ages from Julius Caesar to Winston Churchill to John F. Kennedy have been self-promoters par excellence.

Let your boss and others know of your successes. And always put your accomplishments in writing. Forward brief memos relating your successful completion of projects under the guise of keeping your boss up-to-date. Creating a written record of your achievements will serve you well at review time. In most organizations, when something is in writing it is virtually immortal. (When you have bad news, keep it oral.)

Humility—a deadly corporate sin

Women often have difficulty accepting praise or compliments—whether it's on their personal appearance, a promotion, or a job well done. Some feel compelled to point out the flaws in their accomplishment, or that the work was really simple. Pay attention the next time a male associate receives "kudos" for his work. See if he attributes his accomplishments to luck, or goes out of his way to spread the glory to others. But don't hold your breath waiting!

Humility and slow career progress go hand-in-hand. If you are praised for your performance, don't downplay your efforts. Leave the modesty to the Oscar winners. Just remember that most people (men, most notably) embellish considerably on their accomplishments. If you are objective or downplay your achievements, others will think even less of you.

The only good idea is one that gives visibility

The only point to a "good" idea in business is to get favorable visibility. The manager with a "hot" idea really doesn't care if his plan brings in millions for the company, unless he is an owner. The real motivation is that the idea may result in a promotion, recognition, or a salary increase.

In some instances, the good ideas will later fail in the implementation stage. Quite a few top executives have proposed ideas that sounded great on paper but ultimately failed. The initiators didn't care. They had long moved on to higher positions, frequently on the basis of the visibility they received when they proposed the plans.

STRATEGY 5: ASSOCIATE WITH THE RIGHT PEOPLE

Business loves winners. If you circulate with people who are successful, others will assume you are also. Seek out the stars at your company. These people are successful for some reason, and by associating with them you may gain valuable insights into what works and what doesn't at your firm. At a minimum, some of their glory may rub off on you.

STRATEGY 6: BECOME AN EXPERT

Make an effort to find an area of business in which you can become the office expert. Then in a low-key manner make your expertise known. You don't have to know everything about the subject. Just more than anyone else in your area. Often, merely having a comprehensive file on the subject is enough to engender the reputation.

Becoming an expert helped college dropout Lew Ranier of Salomon Brothers make a leap from mail clerk to the youngest member of the executive committee and one of the highest paid managing directors of the firm. Just prior to the invasion of high-tech processing techniques for stock and bond trading, Ranier was promoted from mail room to production room supervisor. In this operations position, he saw an opportunity to make a name for himself in a soon-to-be vital project. On his own initiative, he became a computer expert and set up the firm's first computer room. This success brought him a promotion to clerk on the trading floor, where he performed outstandingly. Ranier couldn't trot out impressive academic or business credentials, so he concentrated on developing an essential expertise better than anyone else.

STRATEGY 7: BECOME A TEAM PLAYER

If your company has sports teams, join one. Many have interdivisional competitions. You will make valuable contacts with people in a position to help your career. If you are a strong player you'll find that others will hear about you in a positive light. (Being a winner is always good for your image regardless of the field.)

If you are not adequate in a sport, don't join immediately. You could look silly, or worse, incompetent in front of your business associates. That impression could impinge on your professional image. Also, anyone who takes playtime seriously (and many people do) is not going to appreciate playing with a neophyte. As a woman your good intentions to participate could actually backfire. You never want to seem weak at anything, otherwise your image may suffer. Instead, select a sport at which you have a good chance of competing, and take lessons. Once you can give your instructor a good game, you are ready to play with your colleagues.

STRATEGY 8: DEVELOP AN INTRIGUING HOBBY

Having the "right" or interesting hobbies is another intriguing way to attract favorable attention. John, a recent Harvard MBA at one of the top New York investment houses, was an avid mountain climber since his freshman year in college. During his first vacation on the job, he went to Colorado for a small climb with his college roommate. On the day of his return to work he happened to share an elevator with the firm's executive vice-president and an important client. To his amazement, the v.p. introduced him to the client, and asked him how his "expedition" had gone.

John had only met the vice-president once before, when he first interviewed with the firm. Yet, due to the unusual and "macho" nature of his hobby, John had attracted important high visibility within the organization.

Consider activities that you can cultivate successfully. Especially those which have the appropriate cachet for your company. An old line blue-blood firm, for instance, might be impressed by sailing or equestrian pursuits. A "macho" type company would be intrigued with scuba diving. Look for activities that will provide the "right touch" for your image. Everyone remembers interesting people.

STRATEGY 9: BECOME INVOLVED IN OUTSIDE ACTIVITIES

Consider participating in outside activities, either of a community or industry nature. If your company has a suburban setting, become involved in various community functions. Find associations which may hold special interest for your company. It could be the United Way, the Rotary Club, or others. When you locate the right one, you will undoubtedly find many of your successful colleagues are similarly involved.

On an industry basis, join one or two well-known professional associations. Not networking groups. Select groups that have both men and women, especially those considered heavyweights in your industry. Attend trade seminars and workshops. If you learn something interesting, circulate a memo around the department highlighting what you have learned. Even the most superficial of presentations should provide at least one useful idea. And if it doesn't, make one up.

Look for opportunities to give speeches, especially in circumstances that will get favorable publicity for you and the company in the local paper. There is usually at least one women's business group in most cities, and they may be very interested in your ideas on careers in your industry. Or consider contributing an article to a professional newsletter. Most industries have them. Familiarize yourself with the type of articles they publish and submit one.

The objective with all of these ideas is the same. To distinguish yourself in the minds of those who make the important decisions in the company.

16

MONEY SENSE

You are what you earn

Top 10 executive incomes for 1983 *

		TOTAL PACKAGE
Frederick Smith	Federal Express	$51,544,263
Charles Lazarus	Toys 'R' Us	43,848,061
Roland Assaf	Sensormatic Electronics	7,285,529
Steven Ross	Warner Communications	3,681,073
George Shinn	First Boston	3,532,803
Richard Eamer	National Medical Enterprise	3,444,718
John Laborde	Tidewater	3,213,530
David Mahoney	Norton Simon, Inc.	2,996,036
Thomas Jones	Northrop	2,910,635
Harrington Drake	Dun & Bradstreet	2,545,634

*According to *Forbes* magazine

THE LIST ABOVE is a sample of what ten men think they're managerial skills are worth. Obviously their companies did, too. And at least one of these high-priced talents was paid handsomely to watch the company profits decline. But that didn't phase his sense of self-worth. If these men won't sell themselves short, why should you?

Money, more than any other single factor, is an indicator of individual worth in our society. People generally assume that a person who has money is special. Money connotes power, sex appeal, attractiveness, and social status. In business it's a measure by which everyone is judged. For this reason alone, every professional woman should maximize her salary in any given position.

Unfortunately, when it comes to managing their salary progress many women recoil, choosing instead to find some comforting satisfactions in the sops and placaters that their employers mete out in lieu of "dollars." Some find solace in the fact that they have "important responsibilities." Others, in the personal satisfaction of knowing that they "do their jobs well." Ironically, however, if their salary is not commensurate with their performance claims, others will discount their accomplishments.

An impressive salary, on the other hand, predisposes others to think highly of one. It connotes managerial competence, ability, and ambition. The fact that it may imply certain qualities, however, does not mean that these qualities are present in actuality.

In the workplace, money is the final arbiter of an employee's worth. It is a method of valuation independent of all other factors, such as title or responsibility. A well-paid executive often seems to do no wrong, and his or her ideas are usually met with enthusiasm. But the same ideas, espoused by a low-paid trainee, are often greeted with skepticism, if they are even acknowledged.

The price of being born female

It is a crippling by-product of the "classic" feminine upbringing that women are subconsciously inculcated with the idea that a discussion of money is vulgar and crass. Even today, many women are unprepared to manage their own finances. Although these circumstances are changing, a surprisingly small percentage of women have their own credit.

The result is that some women are at a significant disadvantage when negotiating for a salary or raise. Unlike men, they are often willing to take what is offered. While we are not saying that all women fall victim to this thinking, the problem is quite pervasive.

Numerous studies have shown that men place a far greater value on their time and abilities than women in similar situations. In negotiating with a male candidate, many employers open with a higher figure than they offer women. They know that men, in contrast to women, are reluctant to settle for less than they deem their worth, even if their assessment is completely outside of the realm of reality.

Alex, a graduate of a four-year college business administration program, had spent five years working in Hong Kong for an American medical products company. Like many employees of U.S. companies working in a foreign country, he made a substantially higher salary than his home-based counterparts. When Alex's company merged with another, his job was eliminated. The company offered him a new position at the home office, but at a much lower, though normal, salary. Piqued, Alex declined the offer.

Alex believed that even in the United States, he warranted his inflated overseas salary. He continued to ask for a salary greater than what people with more extensive credentials and work experience commanded. It took Alex a year of unsuccessful job searching before he decided to lower his salary expectations to a more reasonable level. Such examples of self-inflated market value are much less common with women, who more often than not, undervalue their worth.

BEGINNING THE SALARY GAME: HANDLING JOB OFFERS

The first step in the salary game is knowing your market value. Before interviewing, have a good idea of an equitable salary for your targeted position. When an employer makes you an offer, it should not be the first time you have heard that dollar amount associated with the position.

There are a number of ways to determine an appropriate salary. If you have just graduated from college or business school, your placement office should have records of the entry-level salaries received by students over the past few years. They may even have data on current salary offers. Other sources are alumni working at the company or contacts in similar industries. They may be able to tell you approximately how much candidates at your level are being offered.

Determining standard salary levels is more complicated if you have been working for a few years. Since most people tend to exaggerate their salaries, they are a biased source of information. Executive recruiters, whose business it is to know what salary you can command, are usually more accurate and reliable.

Armed with these statistics you can make an intelligent evaluation of an offer. And then begin bargaining for the best possible amount.

Starving at the bargaining table

Everyone bargains and virtually every offer is negotiable in some form or another. Many companies offer $500 to $1,500 less to a prospective employee than they really expect to pay. This enables the company to "give" a bit when the employee suggests a counteroffer. It makes sense, then, to request more after any first offer.

In salary negotiations don't ever assume that the company representative is being straightforward. Women often fail to accept reality in these situations. When asked their salary expectations (a common interviewing practice), some state what they consider to be a fair figure. This is wrong for two reasons. First, the idea of what is "fair" is often subjected to their almost instinctive, feminine devaluation. Second, one never opens with an actual acceptable amount. It leaves no room for negotiating. If you must reply, always start with a higher figure. In general, though, it is better to get the company to make the first salary proposal.

Keep in mind that your strongest bargaining position is immediately after you have received an offer, but before you have accepted it. According to Richard Thain, Dean of Career Development at the University of Chicago's Graduate School of Business, "The moment they lust for you is the moment that may never come again. That is the time to ask for money. Be specific and explicit in your demands." Use this "power" to your advantage.

Why women are at a disadvantage

There are usually two reasons why many women don't get a competitive salary. First, many fear that the employer will not approve of them. They worry that somehow this "crass" demand for more money will alienate the company, or that it will ruin an otherwise friendly and positive situation. These women are placing more importance on approval than money. Let's face it, approval is nice, but it should be the icing, not the cake.

Second, women are reluctant to ask for more money because they fear being turned down, or, worse, that the offer will be rescinded. Some women feel that since they are fortunate enough to get an offer, they shouldn't risk losing it by "rocking the boat." Both of these attitudes reflect a weak self-image. They also contribute to a psychological power balance that favors the employer at the employee's expense.

THE WORST CASE SCENARIOS   Let's view these concerns objectively. Those who fear alienation of their prospective employer should realize that companies don't see salary negotiations as a personal matter. They will not be offended if you ask for more money. In fact, personnel executives expect people to dicker about offers. They may even lose some respect for you if you don't at least try to get more money. In most situations, you will receive some adjustment since an increase is "built" into the system.

On the other hand, if you accept a low, first-round salary offer, your superiors may begin to wonder if you are as valuable as they originally thought. (If you don't value yourself highly, who else will?) You don't want to put that idea into a prospective boss's head.

One possible outcome to your request is that the employer doesn't meet your counterproposal fully, but does come back with a higher figure. While it may not be as much as you requested, one "go-round" is usually all you can expect from a company unless you are really special or are negotiating for a unique position.

An employer may remain firm at the original offer. When the company refuses to negotiate, it may be that they have a standard starting salary from which they do not deviate. This is often the case with starting salaries at companies hiring freshly-minted college graduates or MBAs. (In this situation companies start individuals with identical backgrounds at the same salary. To do otherwise would result in resentment and attitude problems among peers.) The ball is then in your court to continue to look for a better position or accept the one on the table.

The future is now

You've just been offered a job with a salary that you feel is below your acceptable minimum. You request more money. Instead of an increase, you are assured that while the starting salary may seem low, you will be given substantial raises and by your next promotion you will be getting much more.

Let the employee beware! This ploy is often foisted upon women, although usually not by more reputable companies. It is typically accompanied by the supposedly consoling fact that you will be given lots of opportunities and responsibilities and a chance to really "grow" at the company.

The sad truth is that if you can't get more money at this point, you probably never will. The promise of big salary increases is just that, a promise, usually an empty one. Once you are in the corporate stream, your salary advances will follow standard increments. The corporate routine and norms will not be modified for you. In fact, as soon as you begin the job, any promises about special salary considerations will be promptly forgotten.

As with all negotiations, you have to be ready to "walk." While it will rarely happen, you should be prepared to reject a job offer if the company simply doesn't meet your minimum figure.

Should you ever settle for less money?

After the aggressive salary tactics we've espoused, it might surprise you that we would say "yes." Provided the circumstances are right. Some instances in which you might opt for less money are when:

- You are switching careers and really don't have any solid experience in your proposed field. But don't get caught up in some misguided sense of gratitude because the company offered you a job. They wouldn't have offered you the position if it wasn't to their advantage. (There is no charity in business.) Once you have gained experience, switch companies if the firm is unwilling to bring your salary to an acceptable level.
- You want to work for one of the prestigious training/resume companies. In many instances these firms offer lower starting salaries than others in their field. But the chance to work at them is really invaluable and is one of the few instances in which you should downplay salary considerations. Your next company will pay handsomely for your prestigious credentials.
- You want to enter a field which has intense competition and salaries that are often lower than expected at the lower levels. The creative area of advertising is a good example. You have to be in the race before you can win it.

WINNING THE SALARY GAME: GETTING A RAISE

Once you have a position, your salary quickly becomes the definitive measure by which your superiors judge you. If you have a large salary, you're important in their eyes. If you have a small salary, you're not. Regardless of your perception of your importance to the company, if it doesn't show in your paycheck, then you aren't a key player.

You must move to maximize your salary in any given position, not only for the money, but for its psychological significance. If you have been working for a company for over a year and you have not received a raise, then one is overdue and it's time to take some action.

Perhaps, like many people, you think that you shouldn't have to ask for a raise. Or maybe you entertain Walter Mitty daydreams. You expect that your boss will call you into his office one day, pat you on the back, and say: "The company is proud of your accomplishments. Here's a 30 percent raise."

Unfortunately, such wishful thinking is rarely fulfilled. Even though many companies do have periodic performance reviews, these do not necessarily translate into raises. More often than not, at least some action on your part is required to ensure strong salary increases.

The game strategy

Asking for a raise should not be done lightly or on the spur of the moment. While the rules of the salary game are public knowledge at some companies, at others the entire process is intentionally shrouded in mystery. In some organizations like IBM and Procter & Gamble, just revealing your salary to another employee can be grounds for dismissal. In other organizations, at a minimum it is a serious infraction of the company code.

Despite these difficulties, having an organized game plan greatly increases your chances. Put your plan into effect several months before review time. Since many firms review employee performance on a set schedule, it's easy to plan ahead.

Start by paying attention to job related details. Make sure your performance is free of minor faux pas. Remember, the little errors can have a far greater impact than their trivial nature would indicate. Are you coming to work on time? Is your paperwork properly formatted and free of "typos"? Is your office neatly organized? Now is definitely the time to cut back on the long lunch hours. As silly as it may seem, many an otherwise outstanding career has been sidetracked when the idiosyncrasies of the company were ignored. You simply don't want to give the boss any reason, no matter how trivial, to scuttle your raise.

On another level, initiate a number of important projects that could be completed just prior to salary review time. But don't concentrate on hitting a "home run." Look for several projects that offer a high probability of success, rather than one major assignment that may not get off the ground. Allow yourself a safety margin. You don't want to find yourself in the position of missing a promised deadline just as your salary is being reviewed.

Usually, the decision to give you a raise is based on the input of more than one person. Frequently, it's your boss and his boss, but this is not always the case. Sometimes, the head of the division or department must give the final approval. Knowing who makes these decisions and the standard procedure is essential. Increase your visibility with these key people, subtly and over time.

The most basic problem with asking for a raise is that it may create the spectre of disloyalty in your boss's mind. Either you are being disloyal to him (Why didn't you wait for him to come up with your raise?), or to the organization ("This company has always taken care of its employees.") It may cast a seed of doubt about your long-term prospects at the company. Worse, he may think that you are actively looking for another position, or that you even have another offer in your pocket.

Open your discussion with the boss on a positive note, reaffirming how happy you are with him and the organization. You really can't overemphasize your loyalty at this point.

Other considerations

Obviously you shouldn't ask for a raise right after you've made a mistake that particularly irritated your boss, even if you are due one. Here are some other things to keep in mind.

- Have a realistic grasp of your progress on the job. As one cynical IBM personnel executive put it: "Ninety percent of the people here think that they are in the top ten percent." If your last review was less than positive, make sure that you have demonstrated improvement in those areas your boss specified.
- If you have just been promoted, you should seek a raise as well as the title change. While some companies automatically include a raise with a promotion, not all do.
- Have you just made a major accomplishment in your work? Companies like to keep "hot" employees happy, and at such times you are at your strongest bargaining position.
- If your company has just announced strong business results, timing is good. If it has suffered major business reversals, the signs for a raise aren't auspicious, though they are not completely out of the question.
- Know what constitutes an average raise at your company. Make that figure your minimum, especially if you are currently basking in the glow of success.
- Study your boss for a few days. Has he been in a good mood; has he just received a raise or had a management "pat on the back" for one of his projects? If so, seize the opportunity.

Prepare your case. As with any business proposal, decide your proposed objective (the amount of the raise) and your rationale. Be specific. Then schedule a meeting with your boss and let him know what you want to discuss.

Pick a time when you won't be disturbed. (You don't want to give him any excuse for cutting your meeting short just when you're starting to pin him down.) If your company has regularly-scheduled performance reviews, wait for this meeting. But still be prepared to present and support your case.

Open your discussion with the dollar amount of the raise that you are seeking. (As with all bargaining, ask for more than you think you can get.) Review your accomplishments and show how they were important to the company. If you can point to bottom line increases as a result of your work, by all means do it.

Corporate "blackmail"

Some approaches that you may be tempted to use are best discarded. Your boss is not interested that you "need the extra money." Who doesn't? And, don't whine or complain about your salary. Finally, avoid using that tempting "trump card," a real or bluffed outside offer. While it may seem like a sure-fire tactic to say, "I've got an offer from another company, and if you don't match it, I'll have to leave," you're playing with dynamite.

Many employers consider this approach a form of blackmail, and even if they capitulate and meet your demands, your relationship will never be the same. You will have broken one of the strongest corporate cultural factors, that of loyalty to the organization. Other companies, when subjected to this tactic, will send you on your way with their best wishes. You may be forced to accept the other offer that you really don't want (or don't actually have).

Managerial maneuvers

Despite a strong case on your part, your boss may try to avoid giving you a raise. He may resort to any number of ploys, especially if your performance is deserving of a raise. These range from the company having financial problems, to a busy schedule, to passing the "buck" to a superior.

In these cases be polite, but persistent. If company finances are cited, mention instances where others have been given raises. If you must back down on the actual raise, insist on a commitment for the future. If your boss has to postpone the meeting, get an agreement for another meeting with a specific time.

When the answer is "No"

When your request is rejected, keep your emotions in check. Listen to what your boss is saying. Don't act angry, defeated, or discouraged. Such behavior will backfire. Handle the problem as a professional.

Assess the situation objectively. Are the boss's doubts about your performance justified? If so, discuss how you can demonstrate your improvement. Together, map out a plan for improvement at the end of which he understands you will be asking for a raise.

If the reasons are really not justified, you have two choices. Present your case to upper management yourself. Or begin to look for another job. Since the former strategy is risky, this may be the time to start an aggressive job search. There is no reason to stay in a job if you are not going to be given periodic raises despite satisfactory performance. Frequently, being denied a raise is a sign of dismissal on the horizon— even if in your opinion you have handled your job well.

Any way you look at it, you should be getting periodic raises. If they don't come automatically, ask for them. As long as you do it right, you should be able to avoid negative results. It also shows management that you are confident in yourself and your abilities. And by periodically delineating your accomplishments at these meetings, you will reinforce your image of achievement at the company.

SALARY GAME BONUS: PERKS

When Chrysler was having major financial problems, Lee Iacocca, chairman, gave up his salary and received one dollar a year. But while he chose to give up his salary, he wouldn't part with his corporate perks. From his perspective, he could live without a salary, but not without his perquisites.

Perks are a symbol that cannot be measured by standard monetary comparisons. They connote the significance of the recipient. People have chosen jobs on the basis of the perks that accompany the position: a large expense account, membership in an exclusive club, a chauffered limousine, or access to the company helicopter and jet. In actual dollar value, these perks often cost far less to the company than a salary increase.

Perks become more important the higher you go in an organization. But from entry- to middle-management levels, perks should not be accepted in lieu of a sound salary or a strong raise. Obviously it can be enticing if you work in New York City to have an expense account that enables you to dine free at Lutece or the 21 Club. But when you decide to switch companies, or industries, your low salary can be an albatross around your neck.

It won't be impressive to potential employers if you try to offset your low salary with the fact that you had a restaurant expense account or travel perks. In their view, your base salary is what signifies your real status. Save the perks for your upper-management phase, when they really mean something. At the upper end an executive may be judged far more by the perks that he is accorded than his salary. But at the lower end their value is dubious and diminished by the mere fact that they are given to a lower-level employee.

17

YOU'RE FIRED!

Is there life after termination?

Lee Iacocca	Former president, Ford Motor Co.
William Agee	Former CEO, Bendix Corporation
David Mahoney	Former chairman, Norton Simon, Inc.
Robert Carlson	Former president, United Technologies Corporation
Alexander Haig	Former secretary of state
Lyman Hamilton	Former CEO, ITT
Harding Lawrence	Former chairman, Braniff Airways
Charles Knapp	Former chairman, Financial Corporation of America
James Morgan	Former CEO, Atari
Robert Abboud	Former CEO, First Chicago
Archie McCardell	Former CEO, International Harvester

PRESTIGIOUS PEOPLE with a common bond. Each person on the list has been fired or forced to resign. In fact, many top executives have been fired or forced to move under the implied threat of termination during their careers. Their ensuing success attests to the fact that termination is survivable.

Contrary to prevalent thinking, incompetence is rarely the cause of termination. Regardless of the stated reason, professionals are usually fired because their business style doesn't mesh with that of the boss or the company, not because of the quality or quantity of the work they produce. But whatever the reason, being fired is a traumatic event.

IDENTITY CRISIS

Even top executives, who have had years of noting the vagaries of dismissal, react strongly when they recall their own experiences. "I still flinch when I think about the time I was fired from my first job," relates the senior vice-president of a major chemical company. "It's something you never forget." Or consider Lee Iacocca's description of Henry Ford's efforts to oust him: "In 1975 . . . [Ford] started his month-to-month premeditated plan to destroy me." No matter how strong your ego, you cannot help feeling the effects of termination on your mental outlook, self-image, and confidence.

It is not merely the prospective loss of income that accounts for the psychological effects of termination. Most professionals will find employment quickly and many have a financial cushion to soften the fall. The loss of a job is exacerbated by the fact that for many people their job plays a key role in their identity. A common feeling is if you are fired, then you have no job, and ipso facto, you are a "nobody." For many women, the rejection aspect of termination does the most damage—being told by respected authority figures that they are not wanted any more.

Whatever the psychological implications, it is possible to lessen the impact of termination. The best way is to be prepared mentally. Accept the fact that all positions are interim in nature, and that even if your work is excellent, you can still be fired. (Iacocca certainly had a genius for management in the automobile industry, and yet that didn't stop Henry Ford II from firing him.*)

Never be so sure of yourself or your position that you become oblivious to the signs of your boss's increasing dissatisfaction with you. After being fired from Ford, Iacocca states in his autobiography, "I had always clung to the idea that I was different. . . . And in terms of everything that really counted I was more important than Henry [Ford II]." Always keep a plan in mind if you need to look for a new

---

* When asked why he fired Iacocca, Ford is reported to have said that despite all of the latter's accomplishments at Ford Motor Co., including development of the phenomenally successful Mustang, he "just didn't like the guy."

position quickly. Don't "burn" or drop your contacts with corporate recruiters or potential employers because you believe you won't ever need them again.

Knowing the signs that your job is in jeopardy will give you the edge to get another job while you are still employed. Timing in such situations is a critical factor and one that is more controllable than you might think. Of course, you can't decide the time of your termination, but you can anticipate it, and consequently take action while you still have some maneuvering room.

BAD WEATHER AHEAD: THE SIGNS

Since bosses are human, it is virtually impossible for them not to exhibit some signals that they are unhappy with you. Firing is rarely the act of a momentary decision except in the most autocratic of institutions. The process usually extends over several months, starting when the boss first considers the possibility of letting you go, and ending when you get the "boot." It is this time lag that holds the key to your landing on your feet.

The signs of a termination procedure in process are subtle, but they are there for you to see.

- Look for slight changes in the way the boss acts toward you. It may be a different manner or tone, perhaps less warm even in otherwise relaxing situations. Note changes in behavior patterns. Does the boss inexplicably and suddenly have less time for you? Are you left out of meetings on future business strategies? Or dropped from luncheon plans? Often times these slips are not intentional acts, simply subconscious oversights that indicate what is really going on in the boss's mind.
- Your secretary, and especially the division/departmental manager's secretary, are often good barometers of impending "bad weather." Secretaries, especially those with some length of experience, have an uncanny knack for

sensing when someone is in trouble. And often they have access to confidential personnel memos, such as those from your boss documenting his increasing dissatisfaction with you. (Somebody has to type the memos.)

- If your secretary is treating you with less respect, if she is slow to return your memos, or if she is now too "busy" to handle matters that she previously did, your job may be in jeopardy. If you have a somewhat adversarial relationship with your secretary, and many people do, and she seems to be taking satisfaction in your exasperation with her, this is also a bad sign. She's feeling more powerful in relation to you since she knows you're on your way out. She just isn't smooth enough to hide it.

- Another clue is the quality and status of the work you are being assigned. If you had been handling key projects, but now someone else is getting those plum assignments, you could be on the way out. At consulting and accounting firms, a decline in your billable client hours and the prestige of the projects you're assigned are strong indicators of the instability of your position.

- Finally, if your perks have been rescinded suddenly (for instance an expense account cancelled or a company credit card revoked for no apparent reason), consider yourself in trouble.

Of course, any of the above can have an explanation other than impending termination. This is not to suggest that you assume the worst every time the department manager's secretary looks at you "funny." But if you objectively detect a pattern of change in the level of respect you are accorded by the people we've mentioned, it is time to think seriously about your long-term prospects at the company.

Knowing for sure

The reason for the uncertainty and time lag in termination is that in most organizations your immediate superior simply doesn't have the authority to dismiss you without clearance from upper management. He must confer with his boss, or a division manager, and he must document his "case" against you. This termination process lasts at least a month, and sometimes several. In organizations where people constitute the firm's product, such as in consulting firms, it may take as long as six months for the final decision to be made. During this period the forces working against you are building inexorably toward your dismissal.

For many people, the only time they will know unequivocally that they're in trouble is when they're called into the boss's office and fired. If you've developed a good information-gathering network, you should get insight into your problems earlier. One financial analyst learned about his impending termination from a secretary, who roomed with an assistant in the accounting department (where the final paychecks are "cut").

The "007" approach

Another approach, which is not recommended to the weak of heart, is looking through the boss's desk after work or on Sunday. Most supervisors keep copies of their personnel memos in some special file folder. It's usually not that difficult to find out where such files are kept. It may sound as if this is an outrageous invasion of privacy. But in the corporate war, such guerilla tactics are far more common than one would guess.

While, obviously, a memo recommending your termination is a dead giveaway, this is usually the last piece of "paper" that will be generated about you for the file. If you find such a memo, consider your firing imminent, in a day or so. Earlier on in the termination process, you may only find a handwritten set of notes about you.

Of particular concern is a list of your recent transgressions, such as coming in late or botching a project. There is no other explanation for such a negative list other than that the boss is building a case against you. As much as you will

not want to believe it, this is unequivocal evidence of termination in the works. The time frame you are looking at is
weeks to a few months at most, depending upon your organization.

For those less hardy and not inclined to a little subter-
fuge, the only option is to follow your instincts and be attuned to any subtle changes around you. Like so many career
decisions, it's really a judgment call in the end.

YOUR BATTLE PLAN

Once you suspect termination, move quickly. Maintain
control of your behavior. If management thinks you are aware
of their plans, they will move faster than originally planned.
In the corporate mind, such employees must be eliminated
quickly before they can do harm: taking clients or company
documents, spreading malcontent, or disturbing the corporate harmony. Some sadistic managers won't want you to
spoil their "fun" by your resignation; they want to be the
ones to reject you.

Consider the unfortunate NCR executive who returned
from lunch at a restaurant to see his desk and chair in flames
on the sidewalk in front of company headquarters. John
Patterson, the hard-nosed founder of the company, had a clerk
put the furniture from the executive's office onto the street
and douse it with gasoline. It was Patterson's form of the
more typical "pink slip."

Trying to rebuild?

Don't waste your time trying to perform better in your
job once you know you are a "lame duck." Too many people in jeopardy focus all of their energies on turning the situation around. Many magazines and books recommend that
you work harder, talk to your boss, and in general try to
prove yourself. In our opinion, once the termination "thought

process" has begun, it's simply not worth the effort. And we've never seen it work, other than providing a brief respite.

Once your boss has begun the psychological process of firing you, it is difficult to stop it in his mind. It's the first law of Newtonian physics, an object in motion tends to stay in motion. And a decision in motion tends to stay in motion. It requires greater force than you are able to conjure—unless you are at a high level of management and have your own power base to fight the decision. Generally speaking, the odds against you are astronomical. And if you do bring the subject to the surface by a frank discussion with the boss, more than likely all you will accomplish is to effect your immediate dismissal.

A stay of execution

But let's assume for the sake of argument that through superhuman effort and luck, you are able to get a stay of execution. At best, your position in the company is precarious, and most likely you have only succeeded in effecting a stop-gap measure. In the boss's eyes and those of management (he could not fire you without initially presenting a strong case to upper management), you are tarnished. In all likelihood, your boss has been feeding upper management documentation of your "inadequacies" for some time.

As we stated in our discussion of pegging, a negative image is difficult, almost impossible, to change. It colors everything you do. In the perspective of both your boss and management, you have performed unsatisfactorily in the past. They will not expect any measure of success from you in the future. The next time your performance is not up to par, or your style clashes with someone else's, your termination will be effected much more quickly.

Clinging to a tenuous position only prolongs your agony. You will live in constant fear of making a mistake—fearful that any mistake will set the firing back in action. (And those fears are justified.) You will have to work longer and harder just to stay in place. Because of your near termination, the time you spend in your current position and salary level will be longer than average. And consequently, your career will be thrown off course.

Finally, realistically, don't cast "pearls before swine." Why subject yourself to the humiliation of hanging on to a job by your fingernails? Everyone in your company will probably know how close you came to being fired—that's juicy gossip. That fact many even spread to other companies in your industry. And don't discount that your headhunter will eventually hear of your problems. To get the best from executive recruiters you need to convince them that you are a prized commodity, not a loser.

Above all else, a successful executive needs absolute confidence. You can always get another job, but restoring your confidence is much more difficult.

Some fast moves

At the first sign of trouble, contact your headhunter. Do this before you even rewrite your resume—a savvy manager always has a reasonably up-to-date one on hand. Suggest a meeting in a few days, not immediately. You don't want to appear desperate. Act casually and sound confident. Suggest that you might be interested in moving up in the industry. You want to give the impression that you are looking, not to substitute one job for another, but, to accelerate your career.

Talk to friends and associates in the business discreetly and put out "feelers" about available positions. Qualify the jobs you are seeking (challenging, intriguing, fast paced) so that it doesn't look as if you want any job; that's a tip-off that you are having problems. If you have been alert to your boss's change in attitude, and have acted immediately, you should have a month or two of job prospecting before you are fired.

WHY MOST PEOPLE ARE FIRED ON FRIDAY

Friday is a popular day for firing. And, shades of Scrooge, the Christmas holiday is a perennial favorite for terminations. But this is no mere coincidence. It is a carefully calculated move on the part of the company. A person who has been fired is like the plague, infecting other employees with fears about their own jobs. The termination of an employee creates low morale, and it often makes the company look bad, particularly if the individual seemed to have been doing well in the job.

The company wants to get the "tainted" person out of sight and out of mind as soon as possible. Weekends are a good time to handle such messy matters because there are several days before the employees return to work. (Christmas provides an even longer period of time and people are distracted by other things.) Management thinks that the rest of the organization will forget about their former colleague during those few days. (Of course they're wrong, the termination will be the subject of gossip for weeks.)

The "Twilight Zone"

In some companies the firing of an employee takes on the aura of a Rod Serling vignette. The employee, let's say his name is George, is called into the boss's office at the end of the day and kept there until everyone else has left for the weekend. Being a Friday, the chances are good that most people will leave work promptly. While his desk is cleaned out, George is given the word. Then a security guard accompanies the hapless victim, clutching his termination check, out of the building.

When Monday morning comes his desk is clean and sometimes occupied by a new employee. No one in an official capacity mentions George. Or occasionally a succinct statement that he has taken another "opportunity" is offered. For all intents and purposes, poor George has slipped into a time warp. From the company's perspective this is the perfect termination—the employee is swept away neatly and quickly, never to be heard from again. No fuss, no bother.

Grace under pressure

Obviously it's better to move before being fired, both for your resume and your psyche. But what if despite all the advice, you fail to recognize the signs of imminent firing? Suddenly at the end of the day your boss informs you that you are being fired. While your life may pass before your eyes, it's really not the end of the world, unless you treat it as such. In fact, with a little savvy, your career can rebound even more strongly. It starts with the way you handle the situation.

As unpleasant as it may be, you must handle the termination interview with style. If you are to be successful in business you must become a consummate actor and this is one area that will really test your mettle. You may despise your boss, you may feel as if you are being unfairly treated, and you may want to place a curse on him and his family for the next four generations. One word of advice. Don't.

Revenge is the stuff that dreams are made of. And if the opportunity ever presents itself in the future, then exact your price and enjoy it. But right now such thoughts will only obfuscate the real issue, that of your immediate future, and maintaining your credibility through the coming ordeal.

Follow these suggestions and you'll never regret your performance during a termination. A good part of being successful in business is successful posturing. In fact, the best objective for an exit interview is to instill the company with some doubt as to the wisdom of firing you. Many a previously underestimated employee has gained a grudging respect for the manner in which he or she handled being fired.

- Don't bother to argue or debate the merits of your dismissal. It is a fait accompli and you'll gain nothing but contempt or pity for your efforts.
- Never settle immediately upon terms. Companies are very sensitive about letting women go. You will very likely get a better deal if you wait, regain your composure, and then negotiate for a strong settlement.
- Don't jump at the opportunity to resign versus being fired. You could be losing a valuable bargaining chip in gaining a better termination package. Take a few days to weigh the merits of each option.
- Don't make any negative remarks about the person doing the firing or the company in general. Don't whine, complain, or whimper.
- Even if you are afforded the opportunity, don't hang around the office saying fond farewells to the other employees. They are not your friends and your actions will only engender pity or derision.
- Don't take any company records or client lists with you. The company undoubtedly has a policy against this, and to your considerable embarrassment, your possessions may very well be searched when you leave the premises.
- Don't talk to any of your former colleagues until you have a new position. Then call under the guise of interest in how things are going at your old company. Nonchal-

antly, let the word out that you got an even better position. Then forget them and move on.

Instead of concentrating upon the negative, try to get the most out of the situation. In your separation package consider more pay, a travel allowance for looking for a new position, or perhaps extended medical or insurance benefits until you get a new job.

SELECTING A BASE OF OPERATIONS

In most firing circumstances the company wants you out of sight immediately. Occasionally, however, you will be offered a desk and secretarial services while you look for another job. Usually, the office is in a remote part of the building, though in some instances you are allowed to remain in your office or desk. The higher you are in the organization, the more likely that this will be offered. There are arguments for and against accepting this largesse.

From one perspective, this gambit allows you to retain the illusion of still being employed. Potential employers will have your work number. You will have a secretary to answer your phone and handle your correspondence. You won't have to deal with recruiters calling your home number and having a friend, wife, or child answer the phone. And you will still have someplace to go each day; regimentation in your schedule at this point is important.

On the other hand, it can be an ignominious move. You will continue to run into your former colleagues, and everyone will be aware of every day that you are still without a new job. The fact that you are physically on the premises of the company that did not want you will exacerbate your normal feelings of depression and failure following termination. If you make a clean break, you will eliminate all reminders of the dismissal, and consequently may be able to rebuild your confidence and enthusiasm faster.

Scylla and charybdis: resign or be fired?

Often a company will give you an option in the manner of your leaving. Like Ulysses in ancient Greek mythology, you are confronted by two unacceptable alternatives. You can resign or be fired. (There is, unfortunately, never a choice about whether you depart.)

If you resign you waive unemployment benefits. Since virtually every company gives two weeks severance pay automatically, you must decide whether anything additional they offer to resign is worth giving up what could be lifesaving, unemployment monies.

Companies prefer you to resign not because they want you to keep your record clean, but because their unemployment insurance rates climb permanently with every claimant against them. These benefits, which frequently amount to a couple of hundred dollars per week, can last as long as six months depending upon the state in which you reside and your salary.

For your record, this "resignation versus termination" option is an illusion. The company probably will not confirm the details of your leaving. Many employers, wary of expensive lawsuits, will only confirm a former employee's length of service. So consider carefully before you resign. The only benefit of resigning may be to save some wear on your ego.

Negotiating a deal

Assuming that you heard the wheels of the termination process grinding, take the opportunity to learn about your company's severance policy. Companies have programs delineating the amount of severance pay and the type of benefits that they provide to fired employees. Determine the standard severance for your company and your industry.

Negotiate hard for the best deal that you can get. Never settle immediately on terms. Termination is usually distasteful and unpleasant to the company as well as to you. Most are especially touchy about getting rid of professional women. They want you out of there as soon as possible, with a minimum of noise. In many cases that translates into their acquiescence to a stronger settlement.

HOW TO DISCUSS TERMINATION IN A JOB INTERVIEW

One advantage to moving quickly before being fired is that you won't have to deal with this issue. It is considerably easier to get a job while you are still employed. But what if you don't have a choice?

Often, your resume may provide the only clue to the manner of your departure. If you worked for your old company for nine months before being fired, don't try to cover up the termination as it's not believable. On the other hand, if you want to move to another city and have some years of experience at the company that fired you, then you have a reasonable cover story for resigning. (It's difficult to handle a job search effectively from hundreds of miles away.)

People are fired every day, all over the country. While unpleasant, it is a normal occurrence to headhunters and personnel directors at other companies. Often, this is the only way thay have of getting good people. Many companies are notorious for firing people. If you were canned from one of these "revolving door" companies, you are probably joining a long and illustrious list.

Telling the interviewer that you don't know why you were fired, or denigrating your former employers is a serious mistake. Only the most naive would not know why they were fired, and lashing out at a former employer shows a lack of professionalism and maturity. It will only confirm in the interviewer's mind that you don't understand how to play on a team and that the company was right to fire you.

The key to discussing termination is to create a positive impression regarding the situation. Demonstrate that you have learned from the experience and can be a better employee as a result. Everyone can understand making mistakes on the managerial path, but few will be impressed if you refuse to accept any responsibility for your firing, or if you lash out at your former company, boss, or co-workers. Develop a brief, believable story and shoulder some of the blame yourself (even if your boss was impossible). Once you have explained your termination, drop the subject completely.

You can create a more positive impression about your termination in a number of ways. You might tell the interviewer that you were fired for a particular "weakness," one that really isn't that much of a weakness. For example, cite a tendency to devote too much time to certain projects to the detriment of others. Or perhaps you have concentrated your efforts solely on the paperwork aspects of your job, leaving too little time for the people requirements. Then show how you will overcome these easily correctable problems. Confirm to the interviewer that you don't intend to repeat past mistakes. This demonstrates that you are capable of growth, an asset in any company.

A TIME FOR SELF-EVALUATION

If you have been without a job for a while, your immediate inclination is to jump at your first job offer. Don't do it. If you've gotten one job offer, others will come. Be especially careful on this job selection, as your psyche cannot afford two consecutive terminations. Incorporate your previous experiences into any decision on a new job offer. Avoid a position that recreates some of the factors that caused you to do poorly on your previous job.

Wait until you have two or three job offers, then compare them. Now that you have some solid business experience, you should know the importance of fitting in with a company. You should also have a better idea of the type of company that will fit your personality and style.

During this period take the time to reflect on the reason for your termination and more importantly, on your career in general. Are your problems the result of simple naiveté in a first or second job? Or are the actual reasons merely symptoms for a larger career disease? If you were fired for consistent carelessness in your work, for example, perhaps the problem is that you are really not interested in your career choice and your behavior is a subconscious demonstration of this.

Or perhaps your dismissal resulted from an inability to fit in with the corporate culture and the overall personality of your company or industry. If this is the case, perhaps you should consider a career which meshes better with your natural style and talents.

18

CORPORATE MOVES

Wheeling and dealing for jobs

A LARGE CORPORATION can survive a mistake. An individual often can't. I once put a 'hot ticket,' a wunderkind, in a fast-track corporation where he was soon ousted. He hasn't connected since, and he would probably be president of a major American corporation today if he'd never met me." The speaker is Gerard Roche of the well-respected executive search firm Heidrick & Struggles. He is discussing the difficulties in getting the right match between a corporation and an executive candidate.

Even a man who is considered one of the best in the executive search field knows the inherent risks in changing companies. In his illustrious career he has found candidates for a number of top spots. Among his best-known matches are John Sculley and the presidency of Apple Computer, Edward Hennessey and the top spot at Allied Corp., and Robert Frederick and the presidency of RCA. But he has also overseen placements that were disastrous. Maurice Valente traded in his position as executive vice-president at ITT for the second highest position at RCA. He lasted less than six months there.

SETTING YOUR COURSE

A career path is like a cross-country road trip. You choose your destination, and select what appears to be the best route. Along the way you may encounter unexpected detours or perhaps consider a possible shortcut. You may even decide to switch destinations.

On this hypothetical road trip, there are optimum points for changing your route. Digress at the wrong point and you may find that the new route is bumpier and more precarious than the previous one. It may even hinder you instead of accelerating your journey. The same can be said of job changes. There is a right time, and a wrong time, to make a career move.

Obviously, if you believe your current position is in jeopardy, initiate plans to move immediately. But what if your career is moving along smoothly? When (if at all) should you consider changing jobs?

Some executive recruiters recommend frequent job changes as a means to accelerate career progress. They suggest that you can get more money, and progress further by changing positions often. Unfortunately, statistics do not bear out this self-serving advice. In a review of 237 chief executives of the largest U.S. companies by *Dun's Business Month*, 44 percent had worked at the same company for their entire career; 27 percent had worked at one other company; 13 percent had worked at two other companies; and another 16 percent had worked at more than two other companies. Clearly, there are rewards to remaining with one firm or limiting the number of times you change companies.

There are always risks with a job change. You may trade a secure position for one that is tenuous. You may exchange a boss who is merely irritating for one who just made *Forbes'* annual list of the "Ten Toughest Bosses in America." And your mild case of corporate ennui may seem desirable when you find yourself in the midst of a bitter power struggle in your new company. It is unlikely that you will be fully aware of problems within an organization until you have been there for at least a month.

Too frequently, job changes will have a negative effect on your resume. It will dilute the impact of your accomplishments by giving an impression of instability, a very undesirable trait in a manager. When you leave a company, you are giving up valuable assets—including an information base and political alliances that took time and effort to build. You know how your company works, you've seen its flaws and understand its culture.

Moving to a new company will require you to repeat the same time-consuming process from the beginning. And the outcome is a gamble. You may end up in a better situation or it could be worse. From a distance, "the grass is always greener." A closer inspection usually reveals a substantial number of flaws.

The conservative approach

Most career experts affirm that job changing should be approached conservatively. "Job-hopping is not the secret ingredient to career success," says Dr. Roderick Hodgins, former Director of Placement at the Harvard Business School. Instead, consider "changing jobs when a move will produce a maximum return for the risk entailed by the move." In other words, when a change of jobs will accelerate your career to a significant extent compared to not moving.

In any career there are times when a move will expedite upward career progress more than at other times. Take the typical entry-level position for an MBA or college graduate. Someone who moves after a year in such a neophyte position will gain little long-term career benefits, even if the move is from a prestigious training/resume company. At best, the employee will accomplish a lateral transition with a modest increase in salary. In this situation, it makes more sense to remain at the first company, where time and effort has already been invested.

After three or four years in such a job, with at least one promotion, the ambitious professional should be able to parlay that experience into a significant increase in salary, responsibility, and position. The decision to move to another company, then, hinges on whether the benefits are worth the risk.

Many professionals have moved at the beginning of their career solely for more money. (This is often an attempt to offset poor salary negotiations at the person's initial company.) But a 25 percent increase in salary can't compensate for an unpleasant work environment. Most experienced executives place more emphasis on the role of the prospective move in their overall career plans.

Trading in your chips

Knowing when to change jobs, or to "trade in your chips," is not always immediately apparent. But, to the careful observer, there are times when the benefits of moving are optimized. Observe the fast trackers in your own organization. Check the recent history of your company. Determine at what point in their career progress the "hot shots" moved on to other companies and the kinds of positions they got.

As a rule of thumb, during the earlier phases of a career, the best time to move is about a year after a promotion. The logic behind this is simple. You have shown that you are promotable and after a year have developed useful and transferable expertise. More than likely, your boss will expect that you spend much more than just a year in your job before your next promotion. However, a new company will be more likely to give you that promotion immediately, along with a salary increase that is greater than you could expect through the normal in-house review procedures. The bottom line is that, with the right move, you will jump a year or so on your career path.

At higher levels, during the Junior Management and Middle Management Phases, these optimum time periods may vary. Consider moving when you can cut at least a year or two off the normal promotion time to the next step. For example, consider a marketing professional who will typically spend four years to become a brand manager. The next normal promotion, to group product manager, usually requires another three or four years. A job change after two years as a brand manager often can be used to get that promotion immediately.

The less time as a brand manager, the less chance that a move will result in the higher level position. For example, a brand manager looking to move after a year may only be able to get another brand manager spot.

One reason why job-hopping has such allure is that changing positions is a way of by-passing the normal salary review process and getting a large increase (typically over 25 percent) all at once. When scouting for outside talent, companies must be competitive. The economics of supply and demand come into play. Within the organization, however, no such competition exists (frequently employees are unaware of what their peers are making), and most firms can get by with offering modest increases (5 to 15 percent) to their employees at review time.

This traditional raise policy gives rise to an often unsettling situation within the low levels of the organization. When the competition for newly graduating MBAs is particularly intense, market forces push starting salaries up higher than the normal rate of increase within most companies. As a result, at some firms, new MBAs will start at salaries greater than those of individuals from the same school who have worked there for a year or two.

The wrong moves

A company change will have a lasting impact on your career. The effective use of that tactic should play a vital role in your long-term career progress. Never consider moving just because you are bored, you want a little more money, or you think that another company will be free of the day-to-day grind.

Solid, demonstrable career progress is measured in terms of responsibility, title, and monetary gains. Every job move should be accompanied by a measurable increase in these three areas. Accepting a new position for more money without an increase in responsibility or title will impress no one. In the long run that gambit is usually a waste of time given the added effort needed to get on track at the new firm.

HEADHUNTERS AND JOB HUNTING

Once you've been on the job for a year, it's time to cultivate a relationship with a corporate recruiter or, as they are often called, headhunters. If you are satisfied with your current position, you may think that you don't need to make such a contact. Or perhaps you believe that it is too early in your career. But by the logic of the business world, the best time to look for a headhunter is when you don't need one.

A good headhunter will play an important role in your long-term career progress. He or she can bring promising opportunities to your attention, serve as insurance against an unexpected termination, and expedite your job search by ferreting out available positions and setting up interviews when the time comes for your move.

Of course you can get a job on your own, but many companies expect their non-entry level candidates to come via recruiter referral. In fact, direct contact with a prospective employer can diminish your image. It may appear that you are not good at your job, because, as the thinking goes, a headhunter would have found you.

The job placement business

There are many facets to the job placement business. Employment agencies fill non-management and clerical positions and charge the candidate for their services. Executive career guidance/consulting services counsel on job hunting for a hefty fee and may or may not actually arrange interviews. And "executive" recruiters deal with professional business positions, arrange for interviews, and charge the client company, never the individual.

Companies seeking candidates for professional positions usually employ one of two approaches. They may use the services of a specific firm on an exclusive basis, which then conducts a search for appropriate candidates. Or they may file a job opening "listing" with a range of firms, much the same as a real estate company posting "listings" for a home. Any search firm, then, can send in resumes of its candidate-clients to the prospective company.

This is one main reason why many headhunters are anxious to get a copy of your resume. They can stamp their name on it and forward it to personnel departments for immediate filing. If the company should subsequently hire you, as a result of their actions or not, they can claim credit for you, even if it's months later. At the managerial level, this can mean a hefty fee for a few minutes' work.

With the burgeoning of white-collar positions, the executive search business is booming as well. (Consider that the typical search firm commission is 25 percent of the annual salary of the employee placed. And it can be more: Heidrick & Struggles received one-third of Sculley's million dollar first year compensation.)

There are few entry barriers for someone wanting to establish a search firm. Becoming a headhunter requires no special education, licensing, or capital investment requirements. All that is needed is an office and some telephones. In fact, as one recruiter put it, "All you really need is to have some business cards printed saying that you are a recruiter, and you're in business." Consequently, the relatively young industry has attracted many would-be recruiters who are inept, dishonest, and potentially harmful.

ADVANTAGES OF USING A HEADHUNTER

There are a number of advantages to working with a good executive recruiter who has strong industry contacts:

- It is always better to have someone else sing your praises. When another person is extolling your virtues to a prospective employer, it sounds better than when you are citing the same accomplishments and talents. Having a recruiter represent your interests adds greatly to your stature. Many companies expect their candidates to use them.
- A successful recruiter is often privy to job openings and management shifts at specific companies before the firm's own personnel department is made aware of them.
- A good recruiter has a solid grasp of the type of candidate each company is looking for, and your suitability for a specific position. Hence, they can steer you to the right job and help you avoid job traps.
- Often, they will be a valuable source of information in preparing for an interview with a particular firm. They may provide a personality profile of individuals you will be meeting, and delineate the prospective company's culture and style.
- Many recruiters will help to "package" you in a way that will appeal most to prospective companies. Since they are in the business of getting people jobs, their insights into interviewing, resumes, etc., can be quite useful.

The good, the bad, and the outrageous

The most professional recruiters know their candidates well and take a personal interest in each one. They respect the need for confidentiality in client relationships, and take the time to understand the candidate's long-term career plans. They have specific, useful contacts within the industries in which they specialize, and frequently work on an exclusive basis for companies.

A good recruiter is familiar with the various stages of a career in the field they handle, as well as the concomitant qualifications and responsibilities of each level. They have a good grasp of the corporate cultures or business style of various companies, and are able to discuss a candidate's work and experience as if they, themselves, had worked in the industry. (In fact, many have.)

The best recruiters are in the business for the long run, not for immediate returns. They will present you to a limited number of companies where they think you will fit, and only after they have cleared them with you first. They place much more value on their professional reputation than on closing a particular placement. That means they will tell you to postpone a job change if it's not the right time for you, even if it means losing a commission. For example, a headhunter may suggest that you spend another six months to a year at your current company to increase your market value.

Most qualified executive placement firms focus on a few industries and career specialties. One well-known corporate recruiting firm in New York, for example, deals only with people in marketing/advertising. Obviously, if you are interested in investment banking, a recruiter there would not be your best bet. Any firm or individual claiming to place people in more than a few specific industries is probably not good at any of them.

The bad (or merely mediocre)

Mediocre recruiters have little interest in a candidate's personality or job requirements. They rarely, if ever, work for companies on an exclusive basis. They typically ask a few general questions pertaining to the type of job requested and then solicit a copy of the candidate's resume. Their entire focus is on immediate placement rather than how the move fits in with a candidate's overall career progress. The quicker you are placed, the better for them.

Most mediocre recruiters will try to convince you to grab the first job offer you receive. But they are not thinking of you, only themselves. They are eager for you to accept any offer, regardless of the consequences to your career. Since they don't often count on repeat business, the strong possibility of your subsequent dissatisfaction is of little consequence to them.

Carol was a low-level marketing manager working in Manhattan. She was employed with a second-tier marketing organization with a national reputation. After a period of dissatisfaction, she accepted the invitation of a headhunter to interview with other marketing companies. Her headhunter convinced her to take the first offer to come along, from a fourth string marketing company, unknown outside of the metropolitan area. The headhunter allayed Carol's concern about the company's lack of reputation by describing it as a "golden opportunity" to advance in an organization that had little "management depth."

The small family-owned company soon proved to be far from the opportunity that Carol had been led to expect. All marketing decisions were made by the company founder, and were based solely on his personal tastes. In addition, the founder's son fancied himself in the mold of a business czar, and insinuated himself into every part of the organization. Company morale was quite low. She discovered that the company's lack of "management depth" resulted from the fact that no one stayed there for very long.

One year after taking the position, Carol recontacted her headhunter (who had never called to inquire how the job was going), and asked her to locate a new position in a more well-known company. The recruiter pondered theatrically and then told Carol that she would do her best. Then she offered a caveat that it would be very difficult to place her—the more professional companies wanted talent from well-known companies, not obscure family businesses.

Carol found out too late that all her recruiter wanted was a quick placement. Moving Carol from her first company to the family-run concern was easy. But now that she was working at a relatively unknown company, placement would be difficult. Hence, the headhunter was not interested in someone who would require a lot of time and effort.

The outrageous

Unfortunately, there is a third category of headhunters. The outrageous recruiters. These mountebanks are completely unconcerned about matching you with the right company and position. They make their money by dealing in volume, not quality. They are only interested in accumulating resumes (the more, the better), and hoping that through mass mailings, "shotgunning," and other fast and impersonal approaches at least some of their candidates will be hired. They are unconcerned about repeat business, because many do not expect to be in the business for long. But they make a killing while they last.

Outrageous recruiters can harm your career in any number of ways. These recruiters rely primarily on job listings from major companies (rather than personal contacts) and mailing lists. Since your current company is probably included in this comprehensive list, your resume could be forwarded to it through the oversight of a bored or incompetent secretary.

Many a professional has rued the day he or she handed a resume to a headhunter after only casual contact. Particularly when the personnel department at their current company received a copy of the resume a few weeks later.

Another negative to the incompetent recruiter is that you may be sent to interview for positions that are completely inappropriate or obviously above you. (This is an indication that the headhunter was taking a long shot on a bigger commission.) You could arrive only to discover that you are embarrassingly underqualified for the position and that the company is not even remotely interested. Even if you were not at fault, you receive the blame for this slip-up and it could ruin your chances of interviewing there in the future.

A final warning about this category of recruiter. Discretion is often sacrificed for opportunity. It is quite common for such a recruiter to mention a candidate's name, while still conducting a job search for him or her, in an effort to scout up more business at the candidate's firm. The hapless victim of this tactic may not even be aware of this indiscretion until he or she is summoned to the boss's office and confronted with the information.

HEADHUNTER PROTOCOL

Here are some things to keep in mind in dealing with headhunters:

- When you receive an unsolicited call from a recruiter, ask the name of the firm and the person contacting you. Tell them you are quite happy with your job, but that you will keep them in mind. Then after work get the number from information and return the call later if you are interested. This will impress anyone in your office who may overhear your conversation. By returning the call from a listing in the telephone directory you will insure that you are indeed talking to a search firm and not to a "ringer." More than one sneaky boss has had personnel impersonate a headhunter to test the loyalty of a subordinate.

- Keep your discussions completely private. Absolute security is required at all stages of a job search. If you work in a cubicle or if your office does not afford privacy, call from a phone in another area of the company or arrange a call after work hours. Have your headhunter leave messages with your spouse or get an answering machine at home with a remote controller. Avoid calls at work. (Those messages from "Charley" or "Mr. Jones," who then refuses to give a return phone number, won't fool your secretary for long.)

- Never, under any circumstances, send your resume to a recruiting firm before deciding to use their services. That decision should be made only after several discussions and a thorough check of their reputation. Always meet with them at their office to check their facilities. If they occupy one or two spartan rooms in a cheap neighborhood, they may be just beginning or they may be a fly-by-night outfit. In either case, you don't want them.

- Feel free to discuss your credentials with a prospective

recruiter—but never give a copy of your resume. Instead, let them take notes. Remember, once a recruiter has a copy of your resume you relinquish control over it. It could be in the mail to every company from the East to the West Coast before the day is out.

· Never deal with a recruiter who discusses other current client-candidates by name in an effort to impress you. If they reveal such information to you, there is nothing to stop them from being indiscreet about you with others.

· Deal exclusively with recruiters who agree to contact only those prospective employers whom you have mutually agreed upon beforehand.

Locating a good recruiter

The best way to locate a successful and respected recruiter is through the business grapevine. There are usually a few good search firms in each industry. When fast trackers announce that they are moving, find out who placed them. Most people like to talk (and boast) about their new job, the other offers they received, and how they got them.

During the course of these conversations (which may take place at the proverbial "going away" after-work drink), inquire as to the name of their headhunter and their performance. But don't appear too eager or ask more than a couple of questions. Otherwise, your associates will get the idea that you want to change jobs—and by the next day everyone in the company will think you are leaving.

Once you have selected a recruiter who is well-respected and has a track record in your field, set up an appointment to chat. You interview them. You will find that headhunters, even good ones, like to establish themselves in a control position with their clients. They dangle their power (access to jobs and knowledge) to put you in awe and gain your respect. This makes it easier to influence you and get you to do what they want. Don't be swayed.

CONFIDENTIALITY   Secrecy is of paramount importance while shopping around for a new job. Care is required even during your initial contact with a headhunter. This confidentiality problem is apparent when discussing your plans over the telephone. Unless you have a private office, you will more than likely be overheard by your secretary or colleagues.

After a few years in business, you will find that it is very easy to tell when a co-worker is talking to a headhunter. The cryptic phrases and hushed tones of the conversation are a dead giveaway. Not many people will be fooled by those afternoon "dental appointments" either—especially when you are wearing your best interviewing outfit. Something as innocent as using the copying machine on your own, instead of having your secretary do it, can start people thinking.

Nothing will force your hand faster than your company finding out that you are looking for a job. Consequently, you must avoid signaling others that you are actively considering a move, when you are, in fact, months away from the offer stage. Since most professionals will consider several positions over a period of months before they actually move, the possibility of a slip-up is great. (More than one careless job hunter has left the original of their resume in the Xerox machine when making copies.)

Pay attention to all stages of the process, from the initial contact with the headhunter to actually interviewing with prospective employers. Get your headhunter's home phone, and talk in the evening rather than at work. Consider calling in "sick" for a few days and getting a number of interviews under your belt at one time. The common ploy of a half day off for "personal business" doesn't fool anyone.

19

THE BIG TIME

High risk . . . high reward

Two roads diverged in a wood, and I—I took the one less traveled
by, And that has made all the difference. —ROBERT FROST

THEY WERE LOOKING for the fast track. They had the
chutzpah that often seems to be the domain of the young.
They knew how to package themselves and recognized an
opportunity when they saw one. They were the original "Whiz
Kids."

Following World War II, the automobile industry was
burgeoning. But despite that, the Ford Motor Co. was
undergoing severe financial and business difficulties—and on
the verge of collapse. Some top executives were fleeing to
other companies. At the same time, ten young ex-army offi-
cers arrived home in a hurry to catch up on the years they
had missed while fighting the war. They saw Ford as just that
opportunity.

In the now classic story, they offered themselves in a
"package deal" to the then 28-year-old Henry Ford II. In their
telegram-resume they presented their services, on an "all ten,
or none" basis.

Henry Ford also recognized an opportunity when he saw
one, and against the advice of most of his senior executives,
hired them. The ten young men, who included Robert
McNamara, Charles Thornton, and Arjay Miller, revitalized
the ailing company and went on to illustrious careers in the
business and political worlds.

TAKING RISKS

The "Whiz Kids" had talent and skills. And most likely they would have been successful in business had they taken an alternate, and safer route. But they may never have flown as high as they did following their famous turnaround of the Ford Motor Co. That success earned them international fame.

The traditional route for the ten young men would have been to select a company that was doing well. Take an entry-level management position. And slowly and methodically work their way up the organizational path. Instead they went to a company that was foundering and, conceivably, could have collapsed before they made any headway in their careers. Worse still, they could have been forever associated with the company's failure. That was the risk, but they took it. Their gamble paid off handsomely.

No one can fault following expected career paths. But, today the typical career route will most likely bring success at a much slower rate than in the past. In the 1960s, when the economy was solid and growth seemed almost limitless, many companies actively sought people for the fast track. They would select some people with potential, put them in areas of high visibility, and move them quickly into upper management. William Agee was put on this type of fast track, as was David Mahoney. In fact, most of the top executives in business today benefited from the depression era induced scarcity of talent and the extraordinary economic growth of this period.

Times have changed. No really strong economic booms appear to be on the horizon. With some notable exceptions, most industries have entered a period of uncertainty, anticipating at best modest growth prospects ahead. Worse yet, there are more young people in business than ever before due to the "baby boom," and current allure of big business. As a result, companies are moving talent more slowly and deliberately than ever before.

SEIZING AN OPPORTUNITY

But for those who are looking for the fast track in business, the same high risk/high reward strategy employed by the Whiz Kids is paying off today. A troubled company, such as Ford was in the late forties, can offer the same opportunity to shine. Some of the most famous people in business, such as Lee Iacocca, have made their names by turning around troubled companies. But even if you are not at the top, an ailing company may offer the chance to implement dramatic changes and decisions that would never be available to a lower-level manager at a secure, profitable company.

Before plunging headlong into a job with a troubled company, however, take note of one key fact in the Whiz Kids' strategy. Ford may have had problems, but the industry itself was healthy and showed signs of strong growth potential. As a result, the Ford Motor Co. had a good chance of survival. On the other hand, taking a position with an ailing company whose product is heading toward obsolescence will not offer the same success potential. In other words, don't pin your fast track dreams on reviving a dying hula-hoop company.

There are other considerations with this strategy. If the company has a number of competitors it may not be able to rebound despite the health of the industry. In the last few years, some small computer companies have collapsed, particularly under the IBM juggernaut. Another factor is the financial cushion available to the ailing company. In today's environment, a good product is not enough. Money often makes the difference between a company's success or failure. If you are considering a failing company that is operating on a shoestring budget, the chances are slim that it will be turned around without an influx of cash.

Leaving the crowd

Cathleen Black took a different route to the top. Her fast track strategy entailed entering an area of publishing in which she would stand out. Black began her career in advertising sales for *Holiday* magazine and eventually became publisher of *New York* magazine in 1979. She is connected with the revitalization of that magazine in both the financial aspect as well as the editorial content. As a result of her work on *New York* magazine, she was tapped to head the national daily newspaper *USA Today*.

While most women choose the editorial side of publishing, Black opted to work in the business side, where few women are. This move provided access to management visibility and her achievements became well-known.

There are a number of such opportunities available to women today. Many industries have been traditionally dominated by men. But with recent governmental regulation and court decisions, many firms need to incorporate women into their management ranks. As a result, the women who select these organizations can benefit from the visibility, the training, and the nurturing of their careers there.

SEEING THE FUTURE

As the hot areas of business change, so do the high prospect areas of a company. The area of a company which rivets management's attention one year may change the next. But few people look ahead; most only look at the present. Consequently, many who are seeking a fast track will often enter into the current "focus area" of a company. But to those who look to the future and anticipate where a company's chief concerns will be in the coming years, opportunities abound. These prescient managers beat the crowd and carve a special niche for themselves in that future.

In the 1950s, Walter Wriston saw the future and it was

in the overseas operations of Citibank. He noted that many foreign economies were getting stronger and anticipated the coming importance of overseas banking. Following his instincts, he directed his efforts toward developing a solid reputation in that overlooked department. By venturing into an, as yet, untapped area of the bank, Wriston was ready when management's attention inevitably turned to the overseas functions of the bank. Wriston's preeminence in that department later earned him the chairmanship position of Citibank.

In the 1970s, Wriston's successor at Citibank followed the same strategy. Early in his career, John Reed accepted a position in the consumer business area of the bank. At that time his colleagues were all vying for spots in the overseas functions, which were considered the hot areas of the bank. He might have seen his position as a career derailment. But instead, he saw an opportunity, and taking a major risk, Reed advocated expansion of a then-foundering area of the bank. Of course, Citibank's focus ultimately turned to consumer banking and Reed became a star.

The squeaky wheel

In the last three decades, most people who wanted to get to the top of companies entered marketing and finance functions. But in the 1980s American business is changing. The onslaught of "Japan, Inc.," recession, and the preponderance of MBAs and business majors have caused the traditional routes to the top to slow down.

As a result, some savvy thinking young managers are heading to manufacturing facilities instead of corporate headquarters. Their theory is that the new emphasis on cutting manufacturing costs creates opportunities to catch the corporate spotlight. A line manager who understands manufacturing and production operations can implement cost-cutting tactics that will result in large bottom line savings. Accomplish that and you'll be noticed. According to Robert

Hayes, a Harvard professor, "The fast track often fits the squeaky wheel analogy. The squeaky wheel today is the operations function."

A survey done by Heidrick & Struggles, the Chicago-based recruiting firm, in 1983 illustrates this point. Tracking promotions in major corporations for six months they discovered that: of 74 individuals promoted to top positions, 60 came from operations, 11 from finance, 2 from sales and marketing, and one from law. This is a dramatic change from previous years when most people at the top made it through sales and marketing. Many companies are now looking for people with the old-fashioned "hands on" experience to run the company.

The road less traveled

Most MBAs tend to follow the crowd in their choice of companies. The end result is that many firms are overloaded with equally bright, competent, and ambitious professionals—all vying to get ahead. Standing out amidst an array of cookie-cutter young managers is exceedingly difficult. From upper-management's perspective in such a situation there is very little to distinguish one MBA from another.

Consider the advantages of being one of only a handful of people with a graduate degree in business. In such a company, a person with strong credentials would stand out simply because with an MBA, he or she is unique in the company. Visibility is virtually guaranteed under these circumstances. In fact, the MBA would most likely receive very special training and attention. Before you sign up with a firm that routinely hires hundreds of MBAs every year, look at some companies who would see you as special.

Industries in transition

Another strategy to consider in looking for the fast track are industries in transition. Some changes are the result of major technological innovations, such as the computer revolution. Others are the result of changing American lifestyle or demographics, such as products and services catering to "baby boomers" and "yuppies." And some are due to the evolving role of business in the country today. One example of the latter is the banking industry.

While we had some negative remarks to make about banking and its title proliferation, banking could be one of the best places to make a name for yourself in the coming years. In the last decade, banking lost some of its cachet for ambitious young managers, particularly business school graduates. It was often seen as a place where real promotions were orderly, methodical, and slow. But this is about to change.

As a result of recent governmental deregulation, the banking industry will be radically transformed. That means great opportunities for those who oversee the revolution. Banks will be incorporating new and expanded services and aggressively competing with other financial institutions. High-technology experts, marketers, and managers will be in great demand. And in contrast to previous eras, it could be one of the most exciting industries in which to work.

FAST TRACK TIPS FROM A HARVARD PLACEMENT DIRECTOR

In addition to the suggestions we've previously mentioned, Parker Llewellyn, placement director for Harvard Business School, offers some other tips. He advises those looking for the fast track to consider:

- Companies with an increasing market share in a fast growing industry.
- Newly revitalized firms that are just beginning to fill its management ranks.
- Companies which like to keep divisions small, and consequently, the number of divisions and managers keeps growing.

- Corporations which grow through acquisition and franchising.
- Companies which have a preference for reorganization, and change divisional lines frequently.

The cautious need not apply

Of course there is risk involved in seeking the fast track. It's the nature of the game. Virtually every executive who made it to the top took risks. And many will tell you that some of their risks didn't pay off. In fact, most experts agree that the best chief executives are those who were knocked down hard a few times in their career. And then got up.

The same can be true for you. No it isn't as easy as it once was. But then again, nothing is. You have to assess just how important it is to get to the top. And be willing to not only take a chance, but to lose it all. When John Reed pushed Citibank into expansion of its consumer business, he watched as his strategy incurred staggering losses of over $150 million. A more cautious manager would have pulled out as soon as the plan looked as if it were going sour. But then, a more cautious manager would never have become chairman.

INDEX